Public Planet Books

A series edited by Dilip Gaonkar, Jane Kramer,
Benjamin Lee, and Michael Warner

Public Planet Books is a series designed by writers in and outside the academy—writers working on what could be called
narratives of public culture—to explore questions that ur-
gently concern us all. It is an attempt to open the scholarly
discourse on contemporary public culture, both local and
international, and to illuminate that discourse with the kinds
of narrative that will challenge sophisticated readers, make
them think, and especially make them question. It is, most
important, an experiment in strategies of discourse, com-
bining reportage and critical reflection on unfolding issues
and events—one, we hope, that will provide a running narrative of our societies at this particular fin de siècle. Public
Planet Books is part of the Public Works publication project
of the Center for Transcultural Studies, which also includes
the journal *Public Culture* and the Public Worlds book series.

Modern Social Imaginaries

public planet books

Modern Social Imaginaries

Charles Taylor

DUKE UNIVERSITY PRESS   *Durham and London 2004*

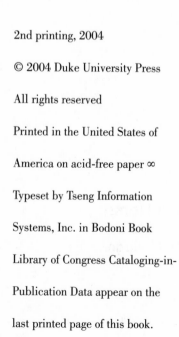

2nd printing, 2004

© 2004 Duke University Press

All rights reserved

Printed in the United States of

America on acid-free paper ∞

Typeset by Tseng Information

Systems, Inc. in Bodoni Book

Library of Congress Cataloging-in-

Publication Data appear on the

last printed page of this book.

To Wanda

Contents

Acknowledgments

First, I want to express my gratitude to the Canada Council for the award of an Isaac Killam Memorial Fellowship for 1996–98, without which I would not have been able to get started on this book as soon as I did.

This work is an expansion of a central section of the book I am preparing on *Living in a Secular Age*, which was the subject of my Gifford Lectures in Edinburgh in 1999.

I want also to mention a debt of another kind. This work emerges out of discussions during the past years at the Center for Transcultural Studies. These discussions have been so central to this book, that one might argue that the Center is a kind of joint collective author of these pages. I especially want to thank Arjun Appadurai, Rajeev Bhargava, Craig Calhoun, Dilip Gaonkar, Nilüfer Göle, Benjamin Lee, Thomas McCarthy, and Michael Warner.

Modern Social Imaginaries

Introduction

From the beginning, the number one problem of modern social science has been modernity itself: that historically unprecedented amalgam of new practices and institutional forms (science, technology, industrial production, urbanization), of new ways of living (individualism, secularization, instrumental rationality); and of new forms of malaise (alienation, meaninglessness, a sense of impending social dissolution).

In our day, the problem needs to be posed from a new angle: Is there a single phenomenon here, or do we need to speak of "multiple modernities," the plural reflecting the fact that other non-Western cultures have modernized in their own way and cannot properly be understood if we try to grasp them in a general theory that was designed originally with the Western case in mind?

This book explores the hypothesis that we can throw some light on both the original and the contemporary issues about modernity if we can come to a clearer definition of the self-understandings that have been constitutive of it. Western modernity on this view is inseparable from a certain kind of social imaginary, and the differences among today's multiple modernities need to be understood in terms of the divergent social imaginaries involved.

This approach is not the same as one that might focus on the "ideas," as against the "institutions," of modernity. The social imaginary is not a set of ideas; rather, it is what enables, through making sense of, the practices of a society. This crucial point is expanded in chapter 3.

My aim here is a modest one. I would like to sketch an account of the forms of social imaginary that have underpinned the rise of Western modernity. My focus is on Western history, which leaves the variety of today's alternative modernities untouched. But I hope that some closer definition of the Western specificity may help us see more clearly what is common among the different paths of contemporary modernization. In writing this, I have obviously drawn heavily on the pioneering work of Benedict Anderson in his *Imagined Communities*,[1] as well as on work by Jürgen Habermas and Michael Warner and on that of Pierre Rosanvallon and others, which I shall acknowledge as the argument unfolds.

My basic hypothesis is that central to Western modernity is a new conception of the moral order of society. This was at first just an idea in the minds of some influential thinkers, but it later came to shape the social imaginary of large strata, and then eventually whole societies. It has now become so self-evident to us that we have trouble seeing it as one possible conception among others. The mutation of this view of moral order into our social imaginary is the coming to be of certain social forms, which are those essentially characterizing Western modernity: the market economy, the public sphere, and the self-governing people, among others.

1 The Modern Moral Order

start with the new vision of moral order. This was most clearly stated in the new theories of Natural Law which emerged in the seventeenth century, largely as a response to the domestic and international disorder wrought by the wars of religion. Grotius and Locke are the most important theorists of reference for our purposes here.

Grotius derives the normative order underlying political society from the nature of its constitutive members. Human beings are rational, sociable agents who are meant to collaborate in peace to their mutual benefit.

Starting in the seventeenth century, this idea has come more and more to dominate our political thinking and the way we imagine our society. It starts off in Grotius's version as a theory of what political society is, that is, what it is in aid of, and how it comes to be. But any theory of this kind also offers inescapably an idea of moral order: it tells us something about how we ought to live together in society.

The picture of society is that of individuals who come together to form a political entity against a certain preexisting moral background and with certain ends in view. The moral background is one of natural rights; these people already have certain moral obligations toward each other. The ends sought are certain common benefits, of which security is the most important.

The underlying idea of moral order stresses the rights and obligations we have as individuals in regard to each other, even prior to or outside of the political bond. Political obligations are seen as an extension or application of these more fundamental moral ties. Political authority itself is legitimate only because it was consented to by individuals (the original contract), and this contract creates binding obligations in virtue of the preexisting principle that promises ought to be kept.

In light of what has later been made of this contract theory, even later in the same century by Locke, it is astonishing how tame are the moral-political conclusions that Grotius draws from it. The grounding of political legitimacy in consent is not put forward in order to question the credentials of existing governments. Rather, the aim of the exercise is to undercut the reasons for rebellion being all too irresponsibly urged by confessional zealots, the assumption being that existing legitimate regimes were ultimately founded on some consent of this kind. Grotius also seeks to give a firm foundation, beyond confessional cavil, to the basic rules of war and peace. In the context of the early seventeenth century, with its continuing bitterly fought wars of religion, this emphasis was entirely understandable.

It is Locke who first uses this theory as a justification of revolution and as a ground for limited government. Rights can now be seriously pleaded against power. Consent is not just an original agreement to set up government, but a continuing right to agree to taxation.

In the next three centuries, from Locke to our day, although the contract language may fall away and be used by only a minority of theorists, the underlying idea of society as existing for the (mutual) benefit of individuals and the defense of their rights takes on more and more importance. That is, it both comes to be the dominant view, pushing older theories of society and newer rivals to the margins of political life and discourse, and it also generates more and more far-reaching claims on political life. The requirement of original consent, via the halfway house of Locke's consent to taxation, becomes the full-fledged doctrine of popular sovereignty under which we now live. The theory of natural rights ends up spawning a dense web of limits to legislative and executive action via the entrenched charters that have become an important feature of contemporary government. The presumption of equality, implicit in the starting point of the state of Nature, where people stand outside all relations of superiority and inferiority,[1] has been applied in more and more contexts, ending with the multiple equal treatment or nondiscrimination provisions, which are an integral part of most entrenched charters.

In other words, during these past four centuries, the idea of moral order implicit in this view of society has undergone a double expansion: in extension (more people live by it; it has become dominant) and in intensity (the demands it makes are heavier and more ramified). The idea has gone, as it were, through a series of "redactions," each richer and more demanding than the previous one, up to the present day.

This double expansion can be traced in a number of ways. The modern discourse of natural law started off in a rather specialized niche. It provided philosophers and legal theorists a language in which to talk about the legitimacy of governments and the rules of war and peace, the nascent doctrines of modern international law. But then it began to infiltrate and transform the discourse in other niches. One such case, which plays a crucial role in the story I'm telling, is the way the new idea of moral order begins to inflect and reformulate the descriptions of God's providence and the order he has established among humans and in the cosmos.

5

Even more important to our lives today is the manner in which this idea of order has become more and more central to our notions of society and polity, remaking them in the process. In the course of this expansion, it has moved from being a theory, animating the discourse of a few experts, to becoming integral to our social imaginary, that is, the way our contemporaries imagine the societies they inhabit and sustain.

Migrating from one niche to many, and from theory to social imaginary, the expansion is also visible along a third axis, as defined by the kind of demands this moral order makes on us.

Sometimes a conception of moral order does not carry with it a real expectation of its integral fulfillment. This does not mean no expectation at all, for otherwise it wouldn't be an idea of moral order in the sense that I'm using the term. It will be seen as something to strive for, and it will be realized by some, but the general sense may be that only a minority will really succeed in following it, at least under present conditions.

Thus the Christian Gospel generates the idea of a community of saints, inspired by love for God, for each other, and for humankind, whose members are devoid of rivalry, mutual resentment, love of gain, ambition to rule, and the like. The general expectation in the Middle Ages was that only a minority of saints really aspired to this and that they had to live in a world that greatly deviated from this ideal. But in the fullness of time, this would be the order of those gathered around God in the final dispensation. We can speak of a moral order here, and not just a gratuitous ideal, because it is thought to be in the process of full realization. But the time for this is not yet.

A distant analogy in another context would be some modern definitions of utopia, which refer us to a way of things that may be realized in some eventually possible conditions, but that meanwhile serve as a standard to steer by.

Rather different from this are the orders that demand a more or less full realization here and now. This can be understood in two ways. In one, the order is held to be realized; it underlies the normal way of things. Medieval conceptions of political order were often of this kind. In the understanding of the "king's two bodies," his individual biological existence realizes and instantiates an undying royal "body." In the absence of highly exceptional and scandalously disordered circumstances, on the occasion of some terrible usurpation, for instance, the order is fully realized. It offers us not so much a prescription as a key to understanding reality, rather as the Chain of Being does in relation to the cosmos that surrounds us. It provides the hermeneutic clue to understanding the real.

But a moral order can stand in another relation to reality, as one not yet realized but demanding to be integrally carried out. It provides an imperative prescription.

Summing up these distinctions, we can say that an idea of moral or political order can either be ultimate, like the community of saints, or for the here and now, and if the latter, it can either be hermeneutic or prescriptive.

The modern idea of order, in contradistinction to the medieval Christian ideal, was seen from the beginning as for the here and now. But it definitely migrates along a path, running from the more hermeneutic to the more prescriptive. As used in its original niche by thinkers like Grotius and Pufendorf, it offered an interpretation of what must underlie established governments; grounded on a supposed founding contract, these enjoyed unquestioned legitimacy. Natural law theory at its origin was a hermeneutic of legitimation.

But already with Locke, the political theory can justify

revolution, indeed, make revolution morally imperative in certain circumstances; at the same time, other general features of the human moral predicament provide a hermeneutic of legitimacy in relation to, for instance, property. Later on down the line, this notion of order will be woven into redactions demanding even more revolutionary changes, including in relations of property, as reflected in influential theories such as those of Rousseau and Marx, for instance.

Thus, while moving from one niche to many and migrating from theory into social imaginary, the modern idea of order also travels on a third axis and the discourses it generates are strung out along the path from the hermeneutic to the prescriptive. In the process, it comes to be intricated with a wide range of ethical concepts, but the resulting amalgams have in common that they make essential use of this understanding of political and moral order that descends from modern natural law theory.

This three-axis expansion is certainly remarkable. It cries out for explanation; unfortunately, it is not part of my rather narrowly focused intentions to offer a causal explanation of the rise of the modern social imaginary. I will be happy if I can clarify somewhat the forms it has taken. But this by its very nature will help to focus more sharply the issues of causal explanation, on which I offer some random thoughts later. For the moment, I want to explore further the peculiar features of this modern order.

A crucial point that ought to be evident from the foregoing is that the notion of moral order I am using goes beyond some proposed schedule of norms that ought to govern our mutual relations and/or political life. What an understanding of moral order adds to an awareness and acceptance of norms is an identification of features of the world or divine action or human life that make certain norms both right and (up to the point indicated) realizable. In other words, the image of order carries a definition not only of what is right, but of the context in which it makes sense to strive for and hope to realize the right (at least partially).

It is clear that the images of moral order that descend through a series of transformations from that inscribed in the natural law theories of Grotius and Locke are rather different from those embedded in the social imaginary of the premodern age. Two important types of premodern moral order are worth singling out here, because we can see them being gradually taken over, displaced, or marginalized by the Grotian-Lockean strand during the transition to political modernity. One is based on the idea of the Law of a people, which has governed this people since time out of mind and which, in a sense, defines it as a people. This idea seems to have been widespread among the Indo-European tribes who at various stages erupted into Europe. It was very powerful in seventeenth-century England under the guise of the Ancient Constitution and became one of the key justifying ideas of the rebellion against the king.[2]

This case should be enough to show that these notions are not always conservative in import. But we should also include in this category the sense of normative order that seems to have been carried on through generations in peasant communities and out of which they developed a picture of the "moral economy," from which they could criticize the burdens laid on them by landlords or the exactions levied on them by state and church.[3] Here again, the recurring idea seems to have been that an original acceptable distribution of burdens had been displaced by usurpation and ought to be rolled back.

The other type of moral order is organized around a notion of a hierarchy in society that expresses and corresponds to a hierarchy in the cosmos. These were often theorized in language drawn from the Platonic-Aristotelian concept of Form, but the underlying notion also emerges strongly in theories of correspondence: for example, the king is in his kingdom as the lion among animals, the eagle among birds, and so on. It is out of this view that the idea emerges that disorders in the human realm will resonate in nature, because the very order of things is threatened. The night on which Duncan was murdered was disturbed by "lamenting heard i' the air; strange screams of death," and it remained dark even though day should have started. On the previous Tuesday, a falcon had been killed by a mousing owl and Duncan's horses turned wild in the night, "Contending 'gainst obedience, as they would / Make war with mankind."[4]

10   In both these cases, particularly in the second, we have an order that tends to impose itself by the course of things; violations are met with a backlash that transcends the merely human realm. This seems to be a very common feature in premodern ideas of moral order. Anaximander likens any deviation from the course of nature to injustice, and says that whatever resists nature must eventually "pay penalty and retribution to each other for their injustice according to the assessment of time."[5] Heraclitus speaks of the order of things in similar terms, when he says that if ever the sun should deviate from its appointed course, the Furies would seize it and drag it back.[6] And of course, the Platonic Forms are active in shaping the things and events in the world of change.

In these cases, it is very clear that a moral order is more than just a set of norms; it also contains what we might call an "ontic" component, identifying features of the world that make the norms realizable. The modern order that descends from Grotius and Locke is not self-realizing in the sense invoked by Hesiod or Plato or the cosmic reactions to Duncan's murder. It is therefore tempting to think that our modern notions of moral order lack altogether an ontic component. But this would be a mistake. There is an important difference, but it lies in the fact that this component is now a feature about us humans, rather than one touching God or the cosmos, and not in the supposed absence altogether of an ontic dimension.

What is peculiar to our modern understanding of order stands out most clearly if we focus on how the idealizations of natural law theory differ from those that were dominant before. Premodern social imaginaries, especially those of the hierarchical type, were structured by various modes of hierarchical complementarity. Society was seen as made up of different orders. These needed and complemented each other, but this didn't mean that their relations were truly mutual, because they didn't exist on the same level. Rather, they formed a hierarchy in which some had greater dignity and value than others. An example is the often repeated medieval idealization of the society of three orders: *oratores, bellatores, laboratores* — those who pray, those who fight, and those who work. It was clear that each needed the others, but there is no doubt that we have here a descending scale of dignity; some functions were in their essence higher than others.

It is crucial to this kind of ideal that the distribution of functions is itself a key part of the normative order. It is not just that each order ought to perform its characteristic function for the others, granted they have entered these relations of exchange, while we keep the possibility open that things might be arranged rather differently (e.g., in a world where everyone does some praying, some fighting, and some working). No, the hierarchical differentiation itself is seen as the proper order of things. It was part of the nature or form of society. In the Platonic and Neoplatonic traditions, this form was already at work in the world, and any attempt to deviate from it turned reality against itself. Society would be denatured in the attempt. Hence the tremendous power of the organic metaphor in these earlier theories. The organism seems the paradigm locus of forms at work, striving to heal its wounds and cure its maladies. At the same time, the arrangement of functions that it exhibits is not simply contingent; it is "normal" and right. That the feet are below the head is how it should be.

The modern idealization of order departs radically from this. It is not just that there is no place for a Platonic-type Form at work: connected to this, whatever distribution of functions a society might develop is deemed contingent; it will be justified or not instrumentally; it cannot itself define the good. The basic normative principle is, indeed, that the members of society serve each other's needs, help each other, in short, behave like the rational and sociable creatures they are. In this way, they complement each other. But the particular functional differentiation they need to take on to do this most effectively is endowed with no essential worth. It is adventitious and potentially changeable. In some cases, it may be merely temporary, as with the principle of the ancient polis, that we may be rulers and ruled in turn. In other cases, it requires lifetime specialization, but there is no inherent value in this and all callings are equal in the sight of God. In one way or the other, the modern order gives no ontological status to hierarchy or any particular structure of differentiation.

In other words, the basic point of the new normative order is the mutual respect and mutual service of the individuals who make up society. The actual structures were meant to serve these ends and were judged instrumentally in this light. The difference might be obscured by the fact that the older orders also ensured a kind of mutual service: the clergy prays for the laity, and the laity defend/work for the clergy. But the crucial point is just this division into types in their hierarchical ordering, whereas in the new understanding, we start with individuals and their debt of mutual service, and the divisions fall out as they can discharge this debt most effectively.

Thus Plato, in book 2I of the *Republic*, starts out by reasoning from the non-self-sufficiency of the individual to the need for an order of mutual service. But quite rapidly it becomes clear that the structure of this order is the basic point. The last doubt is removed when we see that this order is meant to stand in analogy and interaction with the normative order in the soul. By contrast, in the modern ideal, the whole point is the mutual respect and service, however achieved.

I have mentioned two differences that distinguish this ideal from the earlier, Platonic-modeled orders of hierarchical complementarity: the Form is no longer at work in reality, and the distribution of functions is not itself normative. A third difference goes along with this. For the Platonic-derived theories, the mutual service that classes render to each other when they stand in the right relation includes bringing them to the condition of their highest virtue; indeed, this is the service that the whole order, as it were, renders to all its members. But in the modern ideal, mutual respect and service is directed toward serving our ordinary goals: life, liberty, sustenance of self and family. The organization of society, as I said above, is judged not on its inherent form, but instrumentally. Now we can add that what this organization is instrumental to concerns the basic conditions of existence as free agents, rather than the excellence of virtue—although we may judge that we need a high degree of virtue to play our proper part in this.

Our primary service to each other was thus (to use the language of a later age) the provision of collective security, to render our lives and property safe under law. But we also serve each other in practicing economic exchange. These two main ends, security and prosperity, are now the principal goals of organized society, which itself can come to be seen as something in the nature of a profitable exchange among its constituent members. The ideal social order is one in which our purposes mesh, and each in furthering himself helps others.

This ideal order was not thought to be a mere human invention. Rather, it was designed by God, an order in which everything coheres according to God's purposes. Later in the eighteenth century, the same model is projected on the cosmos, in a vision of the universe as a set of perfectly interlocking parts, in which the purposes of each kind of creature mesh with those of all the others.

This order sets the goal for our constructive activity, insofar as it lies within our power to upset it or realize it. Of course, when we look at the whole, we see how much the order is already realized. But when we cast our eye on human affairs, we see how much we have deviated from it and upset it; it becomes the norm to which we should strive to return.

This order was thought to be evident in the nature of things. Of course, if we consult revelation, we also find the demand formulated there that we abide by it. But reason alone can tell us God's purposes. Living things, including ourselves, strive to preserve themselves. This is God's doing:

> God having made Man, and planted in him, as in all other Animals, a strong desire of Self-preservation, and furnished the World with things fit for Food and Rayment and other Necessaries of Life, Subservient to his design, that Man should live and abide for some time upon the Face of the Earth, and not that so curious and wonderful a piece of Workmanship by its own Negligence, or want of Necessities, should perish again . . . God . . . spoke to him, (that is) directed him by his Senses and Reason . . . to the use of those things which were serviceable for his Subsistence, and given him as

the means of his Preservation. . . . For the desire, strong desire of Preserving his Life and Being having been planted in him, as a Principle of Action by God himself, Reason, which was the voice of God in him, could not but teach him and assure him, that pursuing that natural Inclination he had to preserve his Being, he followed the Will of his Maker.[7]

Being endowed with reason, we see that not only our lives but that of all humans are to be preserved. In addition, God made us sociable beings, so that "every one as he is bound to preserve himself, and not quit his Station wilfully; so by the like reason when his Preservation comes not in competition, ought he, as much as he can, to preserve the rest of Mankind."[8]

Similarly, Locke reasons that God gave us our powers of reason and discipline so that we could most effectively go about the business of preserving ourselves. It follows that we ought to be "Industrious and Rational."[9] The ethic of discipline and improvement is itself a requirement of the natural order that God had designed. The imposition of order by human will is itself called for by his scheme.

We can see in Locke's formulation how much he sees mutual service in terms of profitable exchange. "Economic" (i.e., ordered, peaceful, productive) activity has become the model for human behavior and the key to harmonious coexistence. In contrast to the theories of hierarchical complementarity, we meet in a zone of concord and mutual service, not to the extent that we transcend our ordinary goals and purposes, but, on the contrary, in the process of carrying them out according to God's design.

This idealization was at the outset profoundly out of synch with the way things in fact ran, and thus with the effective social imaginary on just about every level of society. Hierarchical complementarity was the principle on which people's lives effectively operated, all the way from the kingdom to the city to the diocese to the parish to the clan and the family. We still have some lively sense of this disparity in the case of the family, because it is really only in our time that the older images of hierarchical complementarity between men and women are being comprehensively challenged. But this is a late stage on a long march, a process in which the modern idealization, advancing along the three axes discussed above, has connected up with and transformed our social imaginary on virtually every level, with revolutionary consequences.

The very revolutionary nature of the consequences ensured that those who first took up this theory would fail to see its application in a host of areas that seem obvious to us today. The powerful hold of hierarchically complementary forms of life—in the family, between master and servant in the household, between lord and peasant on the domain, between educated elite and the masses—made it seem evident that the new principle of order ought to be applied within certain bounds. This often was not even perceived as a restriction. What seems to us flagrant inconsistency, when eighteenth-century Whigs defended their oligarchic power in the name of the people, for instance, was for the Whig leaders themselves just common sense.

In fact, they were drawing on an older understanding of "people," one stemming from a premodern notion of order, of the first type mentioned above, where a people is constituted as such by a Law that always already exists, since time out of mind. This Law can confer leadership on some elements, who thus quite naturally speak for the people. Even revolutions (or what we consider such) in early modern Europe were carried out under this understanding, as, for instance, the monarchomachs in the French wars of religion, who accorded the right to rebel not to the unorganized masses, but to the "subordinate magistrates." This was also the basis of Parliament's rebellion against Charles I.

This long march is perhaps ending only today. Or perhaps we too are victims of a mental restriction, for which our posterity will accuse us of inconsistency or hypocrisy. In any case, some very important tracts of this journey happened very recently. I mentioned contemporary gender relations in this regard, but we should also remember that it wasn't very long ago when whole segments of our supposedly modern society remained outside of this modern social imaginary. Eugen Weber has shown how many communities of French peasants were transformed only late in the nineteenth century and inducted into France as a nation of 40 million individual citizens.[10] He makes plain how much their previous mode of life depended on complementary modes of action that were far from equal, especially but not only between the sexes; there was also the fate of younger siblings who renounced their share of the inheritance to keep the family property together and viable. In a world of indigence and insecurity, of perpetually threatening dearth, the rules of family and community seemed the only guarantee of survival. Modern modes of individualism seemed a luxury, a dangerous indulgence.

This is easy to forget, because once we are well installed in the modern social imaginary, it seems the only possible one, the only one that makes sense. After all, are we not all individuals? Do we not associate in society for our mutual benefit? How else to measure social life?

Our embedding in modern categories makes it very easy for us to entertain a quite distorted view of the process, and this in two respects. First, we tend to read the march of this new principle of order, and its displacing of traditional modes of complementarity, as the rise of "individualism" at the expense of "community." Yet, the new understanding of the individual has as its inevitable flip side a new understanding of sociality, the society of mutual benefit, whose functional differentiations are ultimately contingent and whose members are fundamentally equal. This generally gets lost from view. The individual seems primary because we read the displacement of older forms of complementarity as the erosion of community as such. We seem to be left with a standing problem of how to induce or force the individual into some kind of social order, make him conform and obey the rules.

This recurrent experience of breakdown is real enough. But it shouldn't mask from us the fact that modernity is also the rise of new principles of sociality. Breakdown occurs, as **18** we can see with the case of the French Revolution, because people are expelled from their old forms — through war, revolution, or rapid economic change — before they can find their feet in the new structures, that is, connect some transformed practices to the new principles to form a viable social imaginary. But this doesn't show that modern individualism is by its very essence a solvent of community. Nor that the modern political predicament is that defined by Hobbes: How do we rescue atomic individuals from the prisoners' dilemma? The real, recurring problem has been better defined by Tocqueville, or in our day, François Furet.

The second distortion is the familiar one. The modern principle seems to us so self-evident — Are we not by nature and essence individuals? — that we are tempted by a "subtraction" account of the rise of modernity. We just needed to liberate ourselves from the old horizons, and then the mutual service conception of order was the obvious alternative left. It needed no inventive insight or constructive effort. Individualism and mutual benefit are the evident residual ideas that remain after you have sloughed off the older religions and metaphysics.

But the reverse is the case. Humans have lived for most of their history in modes of complementarity, mixed with a greater or lesser degree of hierarchy. There have been islands of equality, like that of the citizens of the polis, but they are set in a sea of hierarchy once you place them in the bigger picture. Not to speak of how alien these societies are to modern individualism. What is rather surprising is that it was possible to win through to modern individualism, not just on the level of theory, but also transforming and penetrating the social imaginary. Now that this imaginary has become linked with societies of unprecedented power in human history, it seems impossible and mad to try to resist. But we mustn't fall into the anachronism of thinking that this was always the case.

The best antidote to this error is to bring to mind again some of the phases of the long and often conflictual march **19** by which this theory has ended up achieving such a hold on our imagination. I will be doing some of this as my argument proceeds. At this stage, I want to pull together the preceding discussion and outline the main features of this modern understanding of moral order. This can be sketched in three points, to which I then add a fourth:

1. The original idealization of this order of mutual benefit comes in a theory of rights and of legitimate rule. It starts with individuals and conceives society as established for their sake. Political society is seen as an instrument for something prepolitical.

    This individualism signifies a rejection of the previously dominant notion of hierarchy, according to which a human being can be a proper moral agent only when embedded in a larger social whole, whose very nature is to exhibit a hierarchical complementarity. In its original form, the Grotian-Lockean theory stands against all those views, of which Aristotle's is the most prominent, that deny that one can be a fully competent human subject outside of society.

As this idea of order advances and generates new redactions, it becomes connected again with a philosophical anthropology that once again defines humans as social beings, incapable of functioning morally on their own. Rousseau, Hegel, and Marx provide earlier examples, and they are followed by a host of thinkers in our day. But I see these still as redactions of the modern idea, because what they posit as a well-ordered society incorporates relations of mutual service between equal individuals as a crucial element. This is the goal, even for those who think that the bourgeois individual is a fiction and that the goal can be achieved only in a communist society. Even connected to ethical concepts antithetical to those of the natural law theorists, and indeed, closer to the Aristotle they rejected, the kernel of the modern idea remains an *idée force* in our world.

2. As an instrument, political society enables these individuals to serve each other for mutual benefit, both in providing security and in fostering exchange and prosperity. Any differentiations within society are to be justified by this telos; no hierarchical or other form is intrinsically good.

   The significance of this, as we saw above, is that the mutual service centers on the needs of ordinary life, rather than aiming to secure for individuals the highest virtue. It aims to secure their conditions of existence as free agents. Here, too, later redactions involve a revision. With Rousseau, for instance, freedom itself becomes the basis for a new definition of virtue, and an order of true mutual benefit becomes inseparable from one that secures the virtue of self-dependence. But Rousseau and those who followed him still put the central emphasis on securing freedom, equality, and the needs of ordinary life.

3. The theory starts with individuals, whom political society must serve. More important, this service is defined in

terms of the defense of individuals' rights. Freedom is central to these rights. The importance of freedom is attested in the requirement that political society be founded on the consent of those bound by it.

If we reflect on the context in which this theory was operative, we can see that the crucial emphasis on freedom was overdetermined. The order of mutual benefit is an ideal to be constructed. It serves as a guide for those who want to establish a stable peace and then remake society to bring it closer to its norms. The proponents of the theory already see themselves as agents who, through disengaged, disciplined action, can reform their own lives as well as the larger social order. They are buffered, disciplined selves. Free agency is central to their self-understanding. The emphasis on rights and the primacy of freedom among them doesn't just stem from the principle that society should exist for the sake of its members; it also reflects the holders' sense of their own agency and of the situation that agency normatively demands in the world, namely, freedom.

Thus, the ethic at work here should be defined just as much in terms of this condition of agency as in terms of the demands of the ideal order. We should think of it as an ethic of freedom and mutual benefit. Both terms in this expression are essential. That is why consent plays such an important role in the political theories that derive from this ethic.

Summing up, we can say that (1) the order of mutual benefit holds between individuals (or at least moral agents who are independent of larger hierarchical orders); (2) the benefits crucially include life and the means to life, although securing these relates to the practice of virtue; and (3) the order is meant to secure freedom and easily finds expression in terms of rights. To these we can add a fourth point:

4. These rights, this freedom, this mutual benefit is to be secured to all participants equally. Exactly what is meant by equality will vary, but that it must be affirmed in some form follows from the rejection of hierarchical order.

These are the crucial features, the constants that recur in the modern idea of moral order, through its varying redactions.

2 What Is a "Social Imaginary"?

I have used the term "social imaginary" several times in the preceding pages. Perhaps the time has come to make clearer what is involved.

By social imaginary, I mean something much broader and deeper than the intellectual schemes people may entertain when they think about social reality in a disengaged mode. I am thinking, rather, of the ways people imagine their social existence, how they fit together with others, how things go on between them and their fellows, the expectations that are normally met, and the deeper normative notions and images that underlie these expectations.

There are important differences between social imaginary and social theory. I adopt the term imaginary (i) because my focus is on the way ordinary people "imagine" their social surroundings, and this is often not expressed in theoretical terms, but is carried in images, stories, and legends. It is also the case that (ii) theory is often the possession of a small minority, whereas what is interesting in the social imaginary is that it is shared by large groups of people, if not the whole society. Which leads to a third difference: (iii) the social imaginary is that common understanding that makes possible common practices and a widely shared sense of legitimacy.

It often happens that what start off as theories held by a few people come to infiltrate the social imaginary, first of elites, perhaps, and then of the whole society. This is what has happened, *grosso modo*, to the theories of Grotius and Locke, although the transformations have been many along the way and the ultimate forms are rather varied.

Our social imaginary at any given time is complex. It incorporates a sense of the normal expectations we have of each other, the kind of common understanding that enables us to carry out the collective practices that make up our social life. This incorporates some sense of how we all fit together in carrying out the common practice. Such understanding is both factual and normative; that is, we have a sense of how things usually go, but this is interwoven with an idea of how they ought to go, of what missteps would invalidate the practice. Take our practice of choosing governments through general elections. Part of the background understanding that makes sense of our act of voting for each one of us is our awareness of the whole action, involving all citizens, each choosing individually but from among the same alternatives, and the compounding of these microchoices into one binding, collective decision. Essential to our understanding of what is involved in this kind of macrodecision is our ability to identify what would constitute a foul: certain kinds of influence, buying votes, threats, and the like. This kind of macrodecision, in other words, has to meet certain norms if it is to be what it is meant to be. For instance, if a minority could force all others to conform to their orders, the result would cease to be a democratic decision.

Implicit in this understanding of the norms is the ability to recognize ideal cases (e.g., an election in which each citizen exercised to the maximum his or her judgment autonomously, in which everyone was heard). And beyond the ideal stands some notion of a moral or metaphysical order, in the context of which the norms and ideals make sense.

What I'm calling the social imaginary extends beyond the immediate background understanding that makes sense of our particular practices. This is not an arbitrary extension of the concept, because just as the practice without the understanding wouldn't make sense for us and thus wouldn't be possible, so this understanding supposes, if it is to make sense, a wider grasp of our whole predicament: how we stand to each other, how we got to where we are, how we relate to other groups, and so on.

This wider grasp has no clear limits. That's the very nature of what contemporary philosophers have described as the "background."[1] It is in fact that largely unstructured and inarticulate understanding of our whole situation, within which particular features of our world show up for us in the sense they have. It can never be adequately expressed in the form of explicit doctrines because of its unlimited and indefinite nature. That is another reason for speaking here of an imaginary and not a theory.

The relation between practices and the background understanding behind them is therefore not one-sided. If the understanding makes the practice possible, it is also true that it is the practice that largely carries the understanding. At any given time, we can speak of the "repertory" of collective actions at the disposal of a given group of society. These are the common actions that they know how to undertake, all the way from the general election, involving the whole society, to knowing how to strike up a polite but uninvolved conversation with a casual group in the reception hall. The discriminations we have to make to carry these off, knowing whom to speak to and when and how, carry an implicit map of social space, of what kinds of people we can associate with in what ways and in what circumstances. Perhaps I don't initiate the conversation at all if the group are all socially superior to me or outrank me in the bureaucracy or consist entirely of women.

This implicit grasp of social space is unlike a theoretical description of this space, distinguishing different kinds of people and the norms connected to them. The understanding implicit in practice stands to social theory in the same relation that my ability to get around a familiar environment stands to a (literal) map of this area. I am very well able to orient myself without ever having adopted the standpoint of overview the map offers me. Similarly, for most of human history and for most of social life, we function through the grasp we have on the common repertory, without benefit of theoretical overview. Humans operated with a social imaginary well before they ever got into the business of theorizing about themselves.[2]

Another example might help to make more palpable the breadth and depth of this implicit understanding. Let's say we organize a demonstration. This means that this act is already in our repertory. We know how to assemble, pick up banners, and march. We know that this is meant to remain within certain bounds, both spatially (don't invade certain spaces) and in the way it impinges on others (this side of a threshold of aggressivity, no violence). We understand the ritual.

The background understanding that makes this act possible for us is complex, but part of what makes sense of it is some picture of ourselves as speaking to others to whom we are related in a certain way — say, compatriots, or the human race. There is a speech act here, addresser and addressees, and some understanding of how they can stand in this relation to each other. There are public spaces; we are already in some kind of conversation with each other. Like all speech acts, it is addressed to a previously spoken word in the prospect of a to-be-spoken word.[3]

The mode of address says something about the footing we stand on with our addressees. The action is forceful; it is meant to impress, perhaps even to threaten certain consequences if our message is not heard. But it is also meant to persuade; it remains this side of violence. It figures the addressee as one who can be, must be, reasoned with.

The immediate sense of what we're doing, getting the message to the government and our fellow citizens that the cuts must stop, say, makes sense in a wider context, in which we see ourselves as standing in a continuing relation with others, in which it is appropriate to address them in this manner and not, say, by humble supplication or threats of armed insurrection. We can gesture quickly at all this by saying that this kind **27** of demonstration has its normal place in a stable, ordered, democratic society.

This does not mean that there are not cases — Manila 1985, Tianenmen 1989 — where armed insurrection would be perfectly justified. But precisely the point of this act in those circumstances is to invite tyranny to open up to a democratic transition.

We can see how the understanding of what we're doing right now (without which we couldn't be doing *this* action) makes the sense it does because of our grasp on the wider predicament: how we continuously stand or have stood in relation to others and to power. This, in turn, opens out wider perspectives on where we stand in space and time: our relation to other nations and peoples (e.g., to external models of democratic life we are trying to imitate, or of tyranny we are trying to distance ourselves from) and also where we stand in our history, in the narrative of our becoming, whereby we recognize this capacity to demonstrate peacefully as an achievement of democracy, hard-won by our ancestors or something we aspire to become capable of through this common action.

This sense of standing internationally and in history can be invoked in the iconography of the demonstration itself, as in Tianenmen in 1989, with its references to the French Revolution and its citation of the American case through the Statue of Liberty.

The background that makes sense of any given act is thus wide and deep. It doesn't include everything in our world, but the relevant sense-giving features can't be circumscribed; because of this, we can say that sense giving draws on our whole world, that is, our sense of our whole predicament in time and space, among others and in history.

An important part of this wider background is what I called above a sense of moral order. I mean by this more than just a grasp on the norms underlying our social practice, which are part of the immediate understanding that makes this practice possible. There also must be a sense, as I stated above, of what makes these norms realizable. This too, is an essential part of the context of action. People don't demonstrate for the impossible, for the utopic[4]—or if they do, then this becomes ipso facto a rather different action. Part of what we're saying as we march on Tianenmen is that a (somewhat more) democratic society is possible for us, that we could bring it off, in spite of the skepticism of our gerontocratic rulers.

Just what this confidence is based on—for instance, that human beings can sustain a democratic order together, that this is within our human possibilities—will include the images of moral order through which we understand human life and history. It ought to be clear from the above that our images of moral order, although they make sense of some of our actions, are by no means necessarily tilted toward the status quo. They may also underlie revolutionary practice, as at Manila and Beijing, just as they may underwrite the established order.

The modern theory of moral order gradually infiltrates and transforms our social imaginary. In this process, what is originally just an idealization grows into a complex imaginary through being taken up and associated with social practices, in part traditional ones but ones often transformed by the contact. This is crucial to what I called above the extension of the understanding of moral order. It couldn't have become the dominant view in our culture without this penetration/transformation of our imaginary.

We see transitions of this kind happening, for instance, in the great founding revolutions of our contemporary Western world, the American and the French. The transition was much smoother and less catastrophic in one case, because the idealization of popular sovereignty connected relatively unproblematically with an existing practice of popular election of assemblies, whereas in the other case, the inability to translate the same principle into a stable and agreed set of practices was an immense source of conflict and uncertainty for more than a century. But in both these great events, there was some awareness of the historical primacy of theory, which is central to the modern idea of a revolution, whereby we set out to remake our political life according to agreed principles. This constructivism has become a central feature of modern political culture.

What exactly is involved when a theory penetrates and transforms the social imaginary? For the most part, people take up, improvise, or are inducted into new practices. These are made sense of by the new outlook, the one first articulated in the theory; this outlook is the context that gives sense to the practices. Hence the new understanding comes to be accessible to the participants in a way it wasn't before. It begins to define the contours of their world and can eventually come to count as the taken-for-granted shape of things, too obvious to mention.

But this process isn't just one-sided, a theory making over a social imaginary. In coming to make sense of the action the theory is glossed, as it were, given a particular shape as the context of these practices. Rather like Kant's notion of an abstract category becoming "schematized" when it is applied to reality in space and time, the theory is schematized in the dense sphere of common practice.[5]

Nor need the process end here. The new practice, with the implicit understanding it generates, can be the basis for modifications of theory, which in turn can inflect practice, and so on.

What I'm calling the long march is a process whereby new practices, or modifications of old ones, either developed through improvisation among certain groups and strata of the population (e.g., the public sphere among educated elites in the eighteenth century, trade unions among workers in the nineteenth); or else were launched by elites in such a way as to recruit a larger and larger base (e.g., the Jacobin organization of the sections in Paris). Alternatively, in the course of their slow development and ramification, a set of practices gradually changed their meaning for people, and hence helped to constitute a new social imaginary (the "economy"). The result in all these cases was a profound transformation of the social imaginary in Western societies, and thus of the world in which we live.

3 The Specter of Idealism

The fact that I have started this discussion of Western modernity with an underlying idea of order, which first was a theory and later helped shaped social imaginaries, may smack to some readers of "idealism," the attributing to ideas of an independent force in history. But surely, the causal arrow runs in the reverse direction. For instance, the importance of the economic model in the modern understanding of order must reflect what was happening on the ground, for instance, the rise of merchants, of capitalist forms of agriculture, the extension of markets. This gives the correct, "materialist" explanation.

I think this kind of objection is based on a false dichotomy, that between ideas and material factors as rival causal agencies. In fact, what we see in human history is ranges of human practices that are both at once, that is, material practices carried out by human beings in space and time, and very often coercively maintained, and at the same time, self-conceptions, modes of understanding. These are often inseparable, in the way described in the discussion of social imaginaries, just because the self-understandings are the essential condition of the practice making the sense that it does to the participants. Because human practices are the kind of thing that makes sense, certain ideas are internal to them; one cannot distinguish the two in order to ask the question Which causes which?

Materialism, if it is to make any sense, has to be formulated differently, somewhat in the way G. A. Cohen does in his masterful account of historical materialism.[1] It would be a thesis to the effect that certain motivations are dominant in history, those for material things, say, economic ones, for the means to life or perhaps power. This might explain a progressive transformation of the modes of production toward "higher" forms. In any given case, a certain mode would require certain ideas, legal forms, generally accepted norms, and the rest. Thus, it is recognized in Marxist theory that fully developed capitalism is incompatible with feudal conditions of labor; it requires formally (legally) free laborers who can move and sell their labor as they see fit.

The materialist thesis here says that in any such package of mode of production and legal forms and ideas, it is the former that is the crucial explanatory factor. The underlying motivation pushing agents to adopt the new mode also led them to adopt the new legal forms, because these were essential to that mode. The form of the explanation here is teleological, not a matter of efficient causation. An efficient causal relation is supposed and incorporated in the historical account: because the legal forms facilitate the capitalist mode (efficient causation), agents whose fundamental draw was to this mode were induced to favor the new legal forms (even if at first unconscious of what they were doing). This is an in-order-to explanation, or in other words, a teleological account.

It must be said that materialism, as so formulated, becomes coherent, but at the cost of being implausible as a universal principle. There are lots of contexts in which we can discern that the economic motive is primary and explains the adoption of certain moral ideas, as when advertisers in the 1960s adopt the new language of expressive individualism and become eventually inducted into the new ideals. But an account in economic terms of the spread of the Reformation doctrine of salvation by faith is not very plausible. The only general rule in history is that there is no general rule identifying one order of motivation as always the driving force. Ideas always come in history wrapped up in certain practices, even if these are only discursive practices. But the motivations that drive toward the adoption and spread of these packages may be very varied; indeed, it is not even clear that we have a typology of such motivations (economic vs. political vs. ideal, etc.) that is valid throughout human history.

But just because ideas come in such packages, it might be helpful and also might dissipate any unease over idealism to say a little about how the new idea of moral order came to acquire the strength that eventually allowed it to shape the social imaginaries of modernity.

I have already mentioned one context, in a sense the original home of this modern idea of order, in the discursive practices of theorists reacting to the destruction wrought by the wars of religion. Their aim was to find a stable basis of legitimacy beyond confessional differences. But this whole attempt needs to be placed in a still broader context: what one might call the taming or domestication of the feudal nobility, which went on from the end of the fourteenth and into the sixteenth century. I mean the transformation of the noble class from semi-independent warrior chieftains, often with extensive followings, who in theory owed allegiance to the king but in practice were quite capable of using their coercive power for all sorts of ends unsanctioned by royal power, to a nobility of servants of the Crown/nation, who might often serve in a military capacity but were no longer capable of acting independently in this capacity.

In England, the change came about essentially under the Tudors, who raised a new service nobility over the remnants of the old warrior caste that had laid waste the kingdom in the Wars of the Roses. In France, the process was longer and more conflictual, involving the creation of a new *noblesse de robe* alongside the older *noblesse d'épée*.

This transformation altered the self-understanding of noble and gentry elites, their social imaginary not of the whole society, but of themselves as a class or order within it. It brought with it new models of sociability, new ideals, and new notions of the training required to fulfill their role. The ideal was no longer that of the semi-independent warrior, the *preux chevalier*, with the associated honor code, but rather that of the courtier, acting alongside others in advising and serving royal power. The new gentleman required not principally a training in arms, but a humanistic education that would enable him to become a civil governor. The function was now advising and persuading, first colleagues and ultimately the ruling power. It was necessary to cultivate the capacities of self-presentation, rhetoric, persuasion, winning friendships, looking formidable, accommodating, and pleasing. Where the old nobles lived on their estates surrounded by retainers, who were their subordinates, the new top people had to operate in courts or cities, where the hierarchical relations were more complex, frequently ambiguous, and sometimes as yet indeterminate because adept maneuvering could bring you to the top in a trice (and mistakes could precipitate an abrupt fall).[2]

Hence the new importance of humanist training for elites. Instead of teaching your boy to joust, get him reading Erasmus or Castiglione, so that he knows how to speak properly, make a good impression, converse persuasively with others in a wide variety of situations. This training made sense in the new kind of social space, the new modes of sociability, in which noble or gentry children would have to make their way. The paradigm defining the new sociability is not ritualized combat, but conversation, talking, pleasing, being persuasive, in a context of quasi-equality. I mean by this term not an absence of hierarchy, because court society was full of this, but rather a context in which hierarchy has to be partly bracketed because of the complexity, ambiguity, and indeterminacy noted above. One learns to talk to people at a great range of levels within certain common constraints of politeness, because this is what being pleasing and persuasive require. You can't get anywhere either if you're always pulling rank and ignoring those beneath you or so tongue-tied you can't talk to those above.

These qualities were often packed into the term "courtesy," whose etymology points to the space where they had to be displayed. The term was an old one, going back to the time of the troubadours and passing through the flourishing Burgundian court of the fifteenth century. But its meaning changed. The older courts were places where semi-independent warriors congregated from time to time for jousts and hierarchical displays around the royal household. But when Castiglione writes his best-selling *Courtier*, the context is the city-court of the Duchess of Urbino, where the courtier has his permanent abode and where his occupation is advising his ruler. Life is a continuous conversation.

In its later meaning, courtesy comes to be associated with another term, "civility." This too invokes a dense background.

A crucial strand in this story starts from the Renaissance notion of civility, the ancestor of our "civilization," and with much the same force. It is what we have and those others don't, those who lack the excellences, the refinements, the important achievements that we value in our way of life. The others were the "savages." As we can see from the terms, the underlying epitomizing contrast is between life in the forest and life in the city.

The city, following the ancients, is seen as the site of human life at its best and highest. Aristotle had made clear that humans reach the fullness of their nature only in the polis. Civility connects to the Latin word that translates polis (*civitas*); in fact, derivations of the Greek word were also used with closely related sense: in the seventeenth century, the French spoke of an *état policé* as something they had and the *sauvages* didn't. (Later, I discuss the importance of the ideal of "polished" society.)

So part of what this term designated was the mode of government. One must be governed in orderly fashion, under a code of law, according to which rulers and magistrates exercized their functions. Because of the projection onto them of the image of "natural man," savages were held to lack these things. But what they really did lack in most cases were the makings of what we think of as a modern state, a continuing instrument of government in whose hands was concentrated a great deal of power over the society, so that it was capable of remolding this society in important ways.[3] As this state developed, so it came to be seen as a defining feature of an état policé.

The mode of government required by civility also assured some degree of domestic peace. It didn't consort with rowdiness, random and unauthorized violence, or public brawls, either in young aristocratic bloods or among the people. Of course, in early modern times, there was lots of all this. And this alerts us to an important difference between the place civility had in Renaissance discourse and that which civilization holds in ours. As we read in our morning papers about the massacres in Bosnia or Rwanda or the breakdown of government in Liberia, we tend to feel ourselves in tranquil possession of what we call civilization, even though we may feel a little embarrassed to say so out loud. A race riot at home may disturb our equanimity, but we rapidly revert.

In Renaissance times, the elites among whom this ideal circulated were all too aware that it was not only absent abroad, but all too imperfectly realized at home. The common people, though not on the level of savages in America and even being far above the European savage peoples of the margins (e.g., the Irish, the Russians),[4] still had a long way to go. Even the members of ruling elites needed to be subjected to firm discipline in each new generation, as a Venetian law of public education in 1551 proposed.[5] Civility was not something you attained at a certain stage in history and then relaxed into, which is the way we tend to think about civilization.

Civility reflected the transition that European societies were going through from about 1400, which I described above as the domestication of the nobility. The new (or newly recovered) ideal reflected a new way of life. If we compare the life of, say, the English nobility and gentry before the Wars of the Roses with the way they lived under the Tudors, the difference is striking: fighting is no longer part of the normal way of life of this class, unless it be for wars in the service of the Crown. Something like this process continues over four centuries, until by 1800 a normal civilized country is one that can ensure continuing domestic peace and in which commerce has largely replaced war as the paramount activity with which political society concerns itself—or at least shares preeminence with war.

But this change didn't come about without resistance. Young nobles were capable of outbursts of mayhem, carnivals teetered on the thin line between mock and real violence, brigands were rife, vagabonds could be dangerous, city riots and peasant uprisings, provoked by unbearable conditions of life, were recurrent. Civility had to be to some degree a fighting creed.

Ordered government was one facet of civility, but there were others: a certain development of the arts and sciences, what today we would call technology (here again, like our civilization); the development of rational moral self-control; and also, crucially, taste, manners, refinement—in short, sound education and polite manners.[6]

But these developments, no less than ordered government and domestic peace, were seen as the fruits of discipline and training. A fundamental image was of civility as the result of nurture or taming of an originally wild, raw nature.[7] This is what underlies the, to us, striking ethnocentricity of our ancestors. They didn't see their difference from, say, Amerindians as that between two cultures, as we would say today, but as that between culture and nature. We are trained, disciplined, formed, and they are not. The raw meet the cooked.

It is important not to forget that there was an ambivalence in this contrast. Many were tempted to hold that civility enervates us, renders us effete. Perhaps the height of virtue is to be found precisely in unspoilt nature.[8] And of course, there were honorable exceptions to this whole ethnocentric take, such as Montaigne.[9] But the general understanding of those who did think within the contrast wild/tamed, whatever side they came down on, cast the process that brought us from the first to the second as one involving severe discipline. Lipsius defined it as "the rod of Circe which tameth both man and beast that are touched therewith, whereby each one is brought in awe and due obedience where before they were all fierce and unruly."[10] The "rod of Circe" is a great literary image and makes discipline sound easy, but the second part of the phrase indicates that this transformation is a hard slog. Civility requires working on yourself, not just leaving things as they are but making them over. It involves a struggle to reshape ourselves.

So the high Renaissance understanding of courtesy brings

it close to the same age's understanding of civility.[11] This convergence reflects the taming of the aristocracy and the great internal pacification of society under the nascent modern state (external war was a different matter). Both virtues designate the qualities one needs to bring about cohesion in the new elite social space: "By courtesie and humanitie, all socieites among men are maintained and preserved" and "the chiefe signs of civilitie [are] quietness, concord, agreiment, fellowship and friendship." The virtues promoting social harmony and overall peace include, as well as civility, "Courtesie, Gentlenesse, Affabilitie, Clemencie, Humanitie."[12]

The discussion of civility points us to a third facet of the transition to a pacified elite. Civility was not a natural condition of human beings, nor was it easily attained. It required great efforts of discipline, the taming of raw nature. The child embodies the "natural" condition of lawlessness and has to be made over.[13]

So we need to understand the notion of civility not just in the context of the taming of the nobility, but in relation to the much more widespread and ambitious attempt to make over all classes of society through new forms of discipline — economic, military, religious, moral — which are a striking feature of European society from at least the seventeenth century. This transformation was powered both by the aspiration to a more complete religious reform, both Protestant and Catholic, and by the ambitions of states to achieve more military power and hence, as a necessary condition, a more productive economy. Indeed, these two programs were often interwoven; reforming governments saw religion as a very good source of discipline and churches as handy instruments, and many religious reformers saw ordered social life as the essential expression of conversion.

The Puritan notion of the good life, for instance, saw the saint as a pillar of a new social order. As against the indolence and disorder of monks, beggars, vagabonds, and idle gentlemen, he "betakes himself to some honest and seemly trade, and [does] not suffer his senses to be mortified with idleness."[14] This means not just any activity, but one to which he has given himself as a lifetime's vocation. "He that hath no honest business about which ordinarily to be employed, no settled course to which he may betake himself, cannot please God." So said the Puritan preacher Samuel Hieron.[15]

These men are industrious, disciplined, do useful work, and above all can be relied on. They have "settled courses" and are thus mutually predictable. You can build a solid, dependable social order on the covenants they make with each other. They are not tempted to mischief because idleness is the principal breeding ground of all sorts of evils: "An idle man's brain becometh quickly the shop of the devil . . . Whereof rise mutinies and mutterings in cities against magistrates? You can give no greater cause thereof, than idleness."[16]

With such men a safe, well-ordered society can be built. But of course, not everyone will be like them. However, the Puritan project can cope with this difficulty: the godly were to rule; the unregenerate were to be kept in check. The magistrate, as Baxter thought, must force all men "to learn the word of God and to walk orderly and quietly . . . till they are brought to a voluntary, personal profession of Christianity."[17] This was, of course, basically the same as the order Calvin erected in Geneva.

Thus, while the Calvinist Reformation was defining the path to true Christian obedience, it also seemed to be offering the solution to the grave, even frightening social crises of the age. Spiritual recovery and the rescue of civil order seemed to go together.

To put this another way, we can say that while late medieval elites, clerical of course, but with a growing lay component, were developing ideals of more intense devotion and were

coming to demand church reform, members of the same elites
— sometimes others, sometimes the same people — were de-
veloping/recovering the ideal of civility, with its demands for
a more ordered, less violent social existence. There was some
tension between the two but also symbiosis. They came to inflect each other and, indeed, to have an overlapping agenda.

Thus, in this context, there is a complex causal story behind the fact that the ideal of civility develops an active, trans-
formatory agenda. As time goes on, it is undoubtedly powered
by the escalating demand for military, and hence fiscal, power,
and hence economic performance by industrious, educated,
disciplined populations. But it is also partly the result of the
symbiosis and mutual inflection with the agenda of religious
reform, whereby improvement came to be seen as a duty for
itself, as we see with the ethic of neo-Stoicism.

Negatively, it is partly an attempt to fend off real dangers
to social order and partly a reaction to practices such as Carnival and feasts of misrule that had been accepted in the past
but had become profoundly disturbing to those striving for
the new ideals. Here's where the symbiosis with religious reform plays an obvious role again, because this kind of suscep-
tibility to be upset by the display of vice has been very much
a feature of the stringent religious conscience.

We see clear examples from the field of sexual morality.
The Middle Ages in many parts of Europe tolerated prostitution, which seemed a sensible prophylactic against adul-
tery and rape, with all their disruptive consequences.[18] Even
the Council of Konstanz organized temporary brothels for
the large number of participants who flooded into the town.
But the new trends in devotion tended to emphasize sexual
purity and to turn the main focus away from sins of violence and social division, and so the attitude to prostitution
changes. It becomes inconceivable to countenance it, but it is
also deeply disturbing. A sort of fascination-repulsion arises

that expresses itself in widespread and continued efforts to redeem fallen women. One cannot just let this go on; one has to act.

The upshot is that in the early modern period, elites, under the combined force of these two ideals, turn more and more against popular practices along a wide range. Their tolerance for what they see as disorder, rowdiness, and uncontrolled violence diminishes. What previously was accepted as normal is now seen as unacceptable, even scandalous. Already during the sixteenth century, and sometimes continuing afterward, the complex motives I have been describing lead to the launching of four types of programs:

1. New kinds of poor laws are enacted. These involve an important shift, even reversal, from what went before. In the Middle Ages, there was an aura of sanctity around poverty. It was not that this extremely rank-conscious society did not have a healthy contempt for the destitute and powerless at the absolute bottom of the social ladder. But precisely because of this, the poor person offered an occasion of sanctification. Following the discourse of Matthew 25, to help a person in need was to help Christ. One of the things the powerful of that world did to offset their pride and their trespasses was to offer distributions to the poor. Kings did this, as did monasteries, and later also rich bourgeois. Well-off people left a provision in their wills that alms should be given to a certain number of paupers at their funeral, who should in turn pray for the deceased's soul. Contrary to the Gospel story, the prayer of Lazarus, heard in heaven, might hasten Dives to Abraham's bosom.[19]

   But in the fifteenth century, partly as a result of a rise in population and crop failures and a consequent flow of the destitute to the towns, there is a radical change in attitude. A new series of poor laws is adopted, whose principle is sharply to distinguish those who are capable of work from those who genuinely have no recourse but charity. The former are expelled or put to work for very low pay and often in stringent conditions. The incapable poor are to be given relief, but again in highly controlled conditions, which often ends up involving confinement in institutions that in some ways resemble prisons. Efforts are also made to rehabilitate the children of beggars, to teach them a trade, to make them useful and industrious members of society.[20]

All these operations — providing work, relief, training, and rehabilitation — could entail confinement, both as a measure of economy and as a measure of control. This begins the period of what has been called, following Michel Foucault, *le grand renfermement* (the great confinement), which came to involve other classes of helpless people, most famously the insane.[21]

2. National government, city governments, church authorities, or some combination of them, often came down hard on certain elements of popular culture: charivaris, Carnival, feasts of misrule, dancing in church. Here also we see a reversal. What had previously been seen as normal, which everybody had been prepared to participate in, now seemed utterly condemnable and also, in one sense, profoundly disturbing.

Erasmus condemned the Carnival he saw in Siena in 1509 as "unchristian" on two grounds: first, it contained "traces of ancient paganism," and second, "the people over-indulge in licence."[22] The Elizabethan Puritan Philip Stubbes attacked "the horrible vice of pestiferous dancing," which led to "filthy groping and unclean handling" and so became "an introduction to whoredom, a preparative to wantonnesse, a provocative of uncleanness, and an introit to all kinds of lewdness."[23]

As Burke points out, churchmen had been criticizing these aspects of popular culture for centuries.[24] What is new is (a) that the religious attack is intensified, because of the new worries about the place of the sacred, and (b) that the ideal of civility, and its norms of orderliness, polish, and refinement, have alienated the leading classes from these practices.

3. During the seventeenth century, these first two kinds of action become subsumed under a third: the attempts by the developing state structures of absolutist or dirigiste bent, in France and Central Europe, to shape through ordinances the economic, educational, spiritual, and material well-being of their subjects, in the interests of power but also of improvement. The ideal of the well-ordered *Polizeistaat* was uppermost in Germany from the fifteenth to the eighteenth century.[25] The impetus to this dirigiste activity was given by the situation in the wake of the Reformation, in which the ruler of each territory had to see the reorganization of the Church (in Protestant territories) and enforce conformity (in all territories). But the attempts at control are extended in the next century and encompass economic, social, educational, and moral goals. These covered some of the same territory we have already explored: the regulation of relief and the supression of some traditional festivals and practices.[26] But in the sixteenth century, they branch out and try to establish schooling, increase productivity, and inculcate a more rational, hard-working, industrious, and production-oriented outlook in their subjects. Society was to be disciplined, but with the aim of inducing self-discipline.[27]

In short, this meant imposing some features of the ideal of civility on wider and wider strata of the population. Undoubtedly, an important motive here was to create a population from which obedient and effective soldiers could be drawn and the resources to pay and arm them. But many of these ordinances posit improvement (as they see it) as an end in itself. As we move into the eighteenth century, the ends of legislation more and more incorporate the ideas of the Enlightenment, putting increasing emphasis on the productive, material aspects of human activity in the name of the benefits that would accrue to individuals and to society as a whole.[28]

4. We see this whole development from another angle if we look at the proliferation of modes of discipline, of "methods," of procedures. Some of these arise in the individual sphere, as methods of self-control, of intellectual or spiritual development; others are inculcated and imposed in a context of hierarchical control. Foucault notes how programs of training based on the close analysis of physical movement, breaking it down into parts and then drilling people in a standardized form of it, multiply in the sixteenth century. Their primary locus is, of course, armies, which inaugurate new modes of military training, but then some of the principles come to be applied to schools, hospitals, and, later, factories.[29]

Among methodical programs aimed at the transformation of the self, one of the best known was the spiritual exercises of Loyola, meditation directed to spiritual change. But these two key ideas, meditation directed by method, also crop up a century later in the program proposed by Descartes (who was, after all, educated by the Jesuits at Laflèche).

If we take these last two facets together, we see, on the one hand, the development of a new model of elite sociability connected to the notion of civility, in which the paradigm is conversation under conditions of quasi-equality; on the other hand, we see the project of extending this civility beyond the ruling strata to much broader sections of the society. There are affinities here with the modern notion of moral order. Sociability as conversation could suggest a model of society as mutual exchange rather than hierarchical order, whereas the project of transforming nonelites through discipline can mean that the features of civility will not remain forever the property of a single class, but are meant to be spread wider. At the same time, the very goal of making people over suggests a break with the older notions of order, in the semi-Platonic mode of an ideal Form underlying the real and working for its own realization — or at least against whatever infringes it, as the elements expressed their horror at Macbeth's crime. It fits rather with the notion of order as a formula to be realized in constructive artifice, which is just what the modern order offers; societies emerge from human agency through contract, but God has given us the model we should follow.

These are possible affinities, but at the same time, there are others. For instance, society as conversation can give a new relevance to the ideal of republican self-rule, as it did in Renaissance Italy and then later in northern Europe, particularly in England during and after the Civil War.[30] Or it can remain captured within that other agent of social transformation, the "absolute" monarchical state.

What seems to have pushed the elite social consciousness decisively into the ambit of the modern social imaginary were the developments of the new sociability that occurred in the eighteenth century, particularly in England, where they start a little earlier. This period saw a broadening of the elite social stratum, those involved in ruling or administering the society, to include those occupied essentially with economic functions, either because members of the already dominant class turned themselves to these functions, becoming improving landlords, for instance, or because a place was opened for merchants, bankers, and the propertied generally.

The conditions of quasi-equality have to bridge a wider gap. Without engendering the full-scale contemporary notion of equality, the understanding of membership in society was broadened and detached from specific gentry or noble features, even while keeping the language of gentility. The extended understanding of civility, now called "politeness," remained directed to the goal of producing harmony and easing social relations, but now it had to hold together people from different classes and operate in a number of new venues, including coffeehouses, theaters, and gardens.[31] As in the earlier idea of civility, entering polite society involved broadening one's perspective and entering into a higher mode of being than the merely private, but the emphasis now is on the virtue of benevolence and a mode of life less overtly competitive than those fostered by earlier warrior or courtier codes. Eighteenth-century polite society even gave rise to an ethic of "sensibility."

This relative distancing from hierarchy and the new centrality of benevolence brought the age closer to the modern model of order described above. At the same time, the inclusion of economic functions in society intensified the affinity between civility and this notion of order.

This Eighteenth-century transition is in a sense a crucial one in the development of Western modernity. Polite society had a new kind of self-consciousness, which one could call "historical" in a new sense. It was not only unprecedentedly aware of the importance of its economic underpinnings; it also had a new understanding of its place in history, as a way of life that belonged to commercial society, a stage of history recently arrived at. The Eighteenth century generated new, stadial theories of history, which saw human society developing through a series of stages, defined by the form of their economy (e.g., hunter-gatherer, agricultural), culminating in the contemporary commercial society.[32] This made people see the whole transition I have called the taming of the nobility, as well as the internal pacification of modern societies, in a new light. Commerce, *le doux commerce*, was endowed with this power to relegate martial values and the military way of life to a subordinate role, ending their age-old dominance of human culture.[33] Political societies could no longer be understood simply in perennial terms; one had to take account of the epoch in which things happened. Modernity was an epoch without precedent.[34]

4 The Great Disembedding

have offered above one complex context that might help explain the growing force of the modern idea of order, its affinities with the developing understanding of civility, eventually culminating in polite society. But we can also see it in a deeper and longer-term context, that of the "disembedding" of individuals.

One of the central features of Western modernity, on just about any view, is the progress of disenchantment, the eclipse of the world of magic forces and spirits. This was one of the products of the reform movement in Latin Christendom, which issued in the Protestant Reformation but also transformed the Catholic Church. This reform movement was one of the sources of the attempt to discipline and reorder society, described in chapter 3, which aimed not only at the reform of personal conduct but at reforming and remaking societies so as to render them more peaceful, more ordered, more industrious.

The newly remade society was to embody unequivocally the demands of the Gospel in a stable and, as it was increasingly understood, a rational order. This society had no place for the ambivalent complementarities of the older enchanted world: between worldly life and monastic renunciation, between proper order and its periodic suspension in Carnival, between the acknowledged power of spirits and forces and their relegation by divine power. The new order was coherent, uncompromising, all of a piece. Disenchantment brought a new uniformity of purpose and principle.

The progressive imposition of this order meant the end of the unstable postaxial equilibrium. The compromise between the individuated religion of devotion, obedience, or rationally understood virtue, on the one hand, and the collective, often cosmos-related rituals of whole societies, on the other, was broken, and in favor of the former. Disenchantment, reform, and personal religion went together. Just as the church is at its most perfect when each of its members adhere to it on their own individual responsibility—and in certain places, like Congregational Connecticut, this became an explicit requirement of membership—so society itself comes to be reconceived as made up of individuals. The Great Disembedding, as I propose to call it, implicit in the axial revolution, reaches its logical conclusion.

This involved the growth and entrenchment of a new self-understanding of our social existence, one that gave an unprecedented primacy to the individual. In talking of our self-understanding, I am particularly concerned with what I have been calling the social imaginary, that is, the way we collectively imagine, even pretheoretically, our social life in the contemporary Western world.

But first, I want to place the revolution in our imaginary of the past few centuries in the broader sweep of cultural-religious development, as this has generally come to be understood. The full scale of this millennial change becomes clearer if we focus first on some features of the religious life of earlier, smaller-scale societies, insofar as we can trace them. There must have been a phase in which all humans lived in such small-scale societies, even though much of the life of this epoch can only be guessed at.

A focus on what I call early religion (which partly covers what Robert Bellah, for instance, calls "archaic religion") demonstrates in three crucial ways how profoundly these forms of life embed the agent.[1]

First, socially: in paleolithic and even certain neolithic tribal societies, religious life is inseparably linked with social life. Of course, there is a sense in which this is true that is not particular to early religion. This consists in the obvious fact that the basic language, categories of the sacred, forms of religious experience, and modes of ritual action available to agents in these societies are found in their socially established religious life. It is as though each such small-scale society has shaped and articulated some common human capacity in its own original fashion. There have been diffusions and borrowings, but the differences of vocabulary and the gamut of possibilities remain extraordinarily various.

What this common human religious capacity is, whether ontically it is to be placed exclusively within the psyches of human beings or whether the psyche must be seen as responding differently to some human-transcending spiritual reality, we can leave unresolved. Whether something like this is an inescapable dimension of human life or humans can eventually put it behind them we can also leave open (although obviously, the present writer has strong hunches on both these issues). What stands out, however, is, first, the ubiquity of something like a relation to spirits or forces or powers, which are recognized as being in some sense higher, not the ordinary forces and animals of everyday life; and second, how differently these forces and powers are conceived of and related to. This is more than just a difference of theory or belief; it is reflected in a striking difference of capacities and experience, in the repertory of ways of living religion.

Thus, among some peoples, agents fall into trance-like conditions that are understood as possession; among others (sometimes the same ones), powerful portentous dreams occur to certain people, among others, shamans feel themselves to have been transported to a higher world, with others again, surprising cures are effected in certain conditions, and so on. All of these are beyond the range of most people in our modern civilization, as each is beyond the range of other earlier peoples in whose lives this capacity doesn't figure. Thus, for some people, portentous dreams may be possible but not possession; for others, possession but not certain kinds of cure, and so on.

52 Now this fact, that the religious language, capacities, and modes of experience available to each of us comes from the society in which we are born remains true in a sense of all human beings. Even great innovative religious founders have to draw on a preexisting vocabulary available in their society. In the end, this shades into the obvious point about human language in general: that we all acquire it from the language groups we grow up in and can transcend what we are given only by leaning on it. But it is clear that we have moved into a world where spiritual vocabularies have more and more traveled, in which more than one is available to each person, where each vocabulary has already been influenced by many others —where, in short, the rather abrupt differences between the religious lives of people living far from each other are being eroded.

More relevant to the Great Disembedding is a second way in which early religion was social. The primary agency of important religious action—invoking, praying to, sacrificing to, or propitiating gods or spirits; coming close to these powers, getting healing and protection from them, divining under their guidance—was the social group as a whole, or some more specialized agency recognized as acting for the group. In early religion, we primarily relate to God as a society.

We see both aspects of this in, for example, ritual sacrifices among the Dinka, as they were described a half century ago by Godfrey Lienhardt. On the one hand, the major agents of the sacrifice, the "masters of the fishing spear," are in a sense "functionaries," acting for the whole society; on the other hand, the whole community becomes involved, repeats the invocations of the masters, until everyone's attention is focused and concentrated on the single ritual action. It is at the climax "that those attending the ceremony are most palpably members of a single undifferentiated body." This participation often takes the form of possession by the divinity being invoked.[2]

Nor is this just the way things happen to be in a certain community. This collective action is essential for the efficacy of the ritual. You can't mount a powerful invocation of the divinities like this on your own in the Dinka world. This "importance of corporate action by a community of which the individual is really and traditionally a member is the reason for the fear which individual Dinka feel when they suffer misfortune away from home and kin."[3]

This kind of collective ritual action, where the principal agents are acting on behalf of a community, which also in its own way becomes involved in the action, seems to figure virtually everywhere in early religion and continues in some ways up to our day. Certainly it goes on occupying an important place as long as people live in an "enchanted" world—a world of spirits and forces, prior to what we moderns, following Weber, call disenchantment. The medieval ceremony of "beating the bounds" of the agricultural village, for instance, involved the whole parish and could only be effective as a collective act of this whole.

This embedding in social ritual usually carries with it another feature. Because the most important religious action was that of the collective, and because it often required that certain functionaries—priests, shamans, medicine men, diviners, chiefs—fill crucial roles in the action, the social order in which these roles were defined tended to be sacrosanct. This is, of course, the aspect of religious life that was most centrally identified and pilloried by the radical Enlightenment. The crime laid bare here was the entrenchment of forms of inequality, domination, and exploitation through their identification with the untouchable, sacred structure of things. Hence the longing to see the day "when the last king had been strangled with the entrails of the last priest." But this identification is in fact very old, going back to a time when many of the later, more egregious and vicious forms of inequality had not yet been developed, before there were kings and hierarchies of priests.

Behind the issue of inequality and justice lies something deeper, which touches what today we would call the "identity" of the human beings in those earlier societies. Because their most important actions were the doings of whole groups (tribe, clan, subtribe, lineage), articulated in a certain way (the actions were led by chiefs, shamans, masters of the fishing spear), they couldn't conceive themselves as potentially disconnected from this social matrix. It would probably never even occur to them to try.

To get a sense of what this means, we can think of contexts that even for us can't easily be thought away. What would I be like if I had been born to different parents? As an abstract exercise, this question can be addressed (answer: like the people who were in fact born to those other parents). But if I try to get a grip on this, probing my own sense of identity, on the analogy with: what would I be like if I hadn't taken that job? married that woman? and the like, then my head begins to swim. I am getting too deep into the very formative horizon of my identity to be able to make sense of the question. For most people, something like this is also true of their gender.

The point I am trying to make here is that in earlier societies, this inability to imagine the self outside of a particular context extended to membership of that society in its essential order. That this is no longer so with us, that many of these *What would it be like if I were . . . ?* questions are not only conceivable but arise as burning practical issues (Should I emigrate? Should I convert to another religion/no religion?), is the measure of our disembedding. Another fruit of this is our ability to entertain the abstract question even where we cannot make it imaginatively real.

What I'm calling social embeddedness is thus partly an identity thing. From the standpoint of the individual's sense of self, it means the inability to imagine oneself outside a certain matrix. But it also can be understood as a social reality; here it refers to the way we together imagine our social existence, for instance, that our most important actions are those of the whole society, which must be structured in a certain way to carry them out. Growing up in a world where this kind of social imaginary reigns sets the limits on our sense of self.

Embedding thus in society. But this also brings with it an embedding in the cosmos. For in early religion, the spirits and forces with whom we are dealing are in numerous ways intricated in the world. We can see examples of this aplenty if we refer back to the enchanted world of our medieval ancestors: for all that the God they worshipped transcended the world, they nevertheless also had to deal with intracosmic spirits and with causal powers that were embedded in things: relics, sacred places, and the like. In early religion, even the high gods are often identified with certain features of the world, and where the phenomenon that has come to be called "totemism" exists, we can even say that some feature of the world, an animal or plant species, for instance, is central to the identity of a group.[4] It may even be that a particular geographic terrain is essential to our religious life. Certain places are sacred. Or the layout of the land speaks to us of the original disposition of things in sacred time. We relate to the ancestors and to this higher time through this landscape.[5]

Besides this relation to society and the cosmos, there is a third form of embedding in existing reality that we can see in early religion. This is what makes the most striking contrast with what we tend to think of as the "higher" religions. What the people ask for when they invoke or placate divinities and powers is prosperity, health, long life, fertility; what they ask to be preserved from is disease, dearth, sterility, premature death. There is a certain understanding of human flourishing here that we can immediately understand and that, however much we might want to add to it, seems to us quite natural. What is absent, and what seems central to the later, "higher" religions, is the idea that we have to question radically this ordinary understanding, that we are called in some way to go beyond it.

This is not to say that human flourishing is the end sought by all things. The divine may also have other purposes, some of which impact harmfully on us. There is a sense in which, for early religions, the divine is always more than just well-disposed toward us; it may also be indifferent in some ways, or there may also be hostility or jealousy or anger, which we have to deflect. Although benevolence, in principle, may have the upper hand, this process may have to be helped along by propitiation or even by the action of trickster figures. But through all this, what remains true is that divinity's benign purposes are defined in terms of ordinary human flourishing.

Again, there may be capacities some people can attain that go way beyond the ordinary human ones, those of prophets or shamans. But in the end these subserve well-being as ordinarily understood.

By contrast, with Christianity or Buddhism, for instance, there is a notion of our good that goes beyond human flourishing, that we may gain even while failing utterly on the scales of human flourishing, even *through* such a failing (like dying young on a cross), or that involves leaving the field of flourishing altogether (ending the cycle of rebirth). The paradox of Christianity, in relation to early religion, is that it seems to assert the unconditional benevolence of God toward humans (there is none of the ambivalence of early divinity in this respect), and yet it redefines our ends so as to take us beyond flourishing.

In this respect, early religion has something in common with modern exclusive humanism; this has been felt and expressed in the sympathy for paganism of many modern post-Enlightenment people. "Pagan self-assertion," thought John Stuart Mill, was as valid, if not more so, as "Christian self-denial."[6] (This is related to, but not quite the same as, the sympathy felt for polytheism.) What makes modern humanism unprecedented, of course, is the idea that this flourishing involves no relation to anything higher.

Early religion stands in contrast to what many people have called "postaxial" religions.[7] The reference is to what Karl Jaspers called the "axial age,"[8] the extraordinary period in the last millennium B.C.E. when various "higher" forms of religion appeared seemingly independently in different civilizations, marked by such founding figures as Confucius, Gautama, Socrates, and the Hebrew prophets.

The surprising feature of the axial religions, compared with what went before, what would in other words have made them hard to predict beforehand, is that they initiate a break in all three dimensions of embeddedness: social order, cosmos, human good. Not in all cases nor all at once. Perhaps in some ways, Buddhism is the most far-reaching, because it radically undercuts the second dimension: the order of the world itself is called into question because the wheel of rebirth means suffering. In Christianity, there is something analogous: our world is disordered and must be made anew. But some post-axial outlooks keep the sense of relation to an ordered cosmos, as we see in very different ways with Confucius and Plato; however, they mark a distinction between this and the actual, highly imperfect social order, so that the close link to the cosmos through collective religious life is made problematic.

Perhaps most fundamental of all is the revisionary stance toward the human good in axial religions. More or less radically, they all call into question the received, seemingly unquestionable understandings of human flourishing, and hence inevitably also the structures of society and the features of the cosmos through which this flourishing was supposedly achieved.

We might put the contrast this way: unlike postaxial religion, early religion involved an acceptance of the order of things in the three dimensions I have been discussing. In a remarkable series of articles on Australian aboriginal religion, W. E. H. Stanner speaks of "the mood of assent" that is central to this spirituality. Aboriginals had not set up the "kind of quarrel with life" that springs from the various postaxial religious initiatives.[9] The contrast is in some ways easy to miss, because aboriginal mythology, in relating the way the order of things came to be in the Dream Time (the original time out of time, which is also "everywhen"), contains a number of stories of catastrophe, brought on by trickery, deceit, and violence, from which human life recouped and reemerged, but in an impaired and divided fashion, so that there remains the intrinsic connection between life and suffering, and unity is inseparable from division. This may seem reminiscent of other stories of a Fall, including that related in Genesis 1. But in contrast with what Christianity has made of the Fall, for the Aboriginals the imperative to "follow up" the Dreaming, to recover through ritual and insight their contact with the order of the original time, relates to this riven and impaired dispensation in which good and evil are interwoven. There is no question of reparation of the original rift, or of a compensation, or of making good the original loss. Ritual and the wisdom that goes with it can even bring them to accept the inexorable and "celebrate joyously what could not be changed."[10] The original Catastrophe doesn't separate or alienate us from the sacred or higher, as in the Genesis story; rather, it contributes to shaping the sacred order we are trying to "follow up."[11]

Axial religion didn't do away with early religious life. In many ways, features of the earlier practices continued in modified form to define majority religious life for centuries. Modifications arose, of course, not just from the axial formulations, but also from the growth of large-scale, more differentiated, often urban-centered societies, with more hierarchical organization and embryonic state structures. Indeed, it has been argued that these, too, played a part in the process of disembedding, because the very existence of state power entails some attempt to control and shape religious life and the social structures it requires, and hence undercuts the sense of intangibility surrounding this life and these structures.[12] I think there is a lot to this thesis, and indeed, I invoke something like it later on, but for the moment I want to focus on the significance of the axial period.

This doesn't at once totally change the religious life of whole societies. But it does open new possibilities of disembedded religion: seeking a relation to the divine or the higher, which severely revises the going notions of flourishing, or even goes beyond them, and can be carried through by individuals on their own and/or in new kinds of sociality unlinked to the established sacred order. So monks, bhikhus, sanyassi, devotees of some avatar or god strike out on their own, and from this springs unprecedented modes of sociality: initiation groups, sects of devotees, the sangha, monastic orders, and so on.

In all these cases, there is some kind of hiatus, difference, or even break in relation to the religious life of the whole larger society. This itself may be differentiated to some extent, with different strata or castes or classes, and a new religious outlook may lodge in one of them. But very often a new devotion may cut across all of these, particularly where there is a break in the third dimension, with a "higher" idea of the human good.

There is inevitably a tension here, but often there is also an attempt to secure the unity of the whole, to recover some sense of complementarity among the different religious forms. Thus, those who are fully dedicated to the higher forms, though they can be seen as a standing reproach to those who remain in the earlier forms, supplicating the Powers for human flourishing, nevertheless can also be seen in a relationship of mutual help with them. The laity feed the monks and by this they earn merit, which can be understood as taking them a little farther along the higher road, but also serves to protect them against the dangers of life and increases their health, prosperity, and fertility.

So strong is the pull toward complementarity that even in those cases where a higher religion took over the whole society —as with Buddhism, Christianity, and Islam—and there is supposedly nothing left with which to contrast, the difference between dedicated minorities of religious "virtuosi" (to use Max Weber's term) and the mass religion of the social sacred, still largely oriented to flourishing, survived or reconstituted itself with the same combination of strain on one hand and hierarchical complementarity on the other.

From our modern perspective, with 20/20 hindsight, it appears as though the axial spiritualities were prevented from producing their full disembedding effect because they were so to speak hemmed in by the force of the majority religious life that remained firmly in the old mold. They did bring about a certain form of religious individualism, but this was what Louis Dumont called the charter for "l'individu hors du monde" (otherworldly individual).[13] That is, it was the way of life of elite minorities, and it was in some ways marginal to or in some tension with the "world," meaning not just the cosmos that is ordered in relation to the higher or the sacred, but also the society that is ordered in relation to both cosmos and sacred. This world was still a matrix of embeddedness, and it still provided the inescapable framework for social life, including that of the individuals who tried to turn their backs on it, insofar as they remained in some sense within its reach.

What had yet to happen was for this matrix to be itself transformed, to be made over according to some of the principles of axial spirituality, so that the world itself would come to be seen as constituted by individuals. This would be the charter for "l'individu dans le monde" (intrawordly individual) in Dumont's terms, the agent who, in his ordinary worldly life, sees himself as primordially an individual, that is, the human agent of Western modernity.

This project of transformation is the one I described in the previous chapters: the attempt to make over society in a thoroughgoing way according to the demands of a Christian order, while purging it of its connection to an enchanted cosmos and removing all vestiges of the old complementarities — between spiritual and temporal, between life devoted to God and life in the world, between order and the chaos on which it draws.

This project was thoroughly disembedding just by virtue of its form or mode of operation: the disciplined remaking of behavior and social forms through objectification and an instrumental stance. But its ends were also intrinsically concerned with disembedding. This is clear with the drive to disenchantment, which destroys the second dimension of embeddedness. We can also see it in the Christian context. In one way, Christianity here operates like any axial spirituality; indeed, it operates in conjunction with another such, namely, Stoicism. But there also were specifically Christian modes. The New Testament is full of calls to leave or relativize solidarities of family, clan, and society and be part of the Kingdom. We see this seriously reflected in the way certain Protestant churches operated, where one was not simply a member by virtue of birth but had to join by answering a personal call. This in turn helped to give force to a conception of society as founded on covenant, and hence as ultimately constituted by the decision of free individuals.

This is a relatively obvious filiation. But my thesis is that the effect of the Christian, or Christian-Stoic, attempt to remake society in bringing about the modern "individual in the world" was much more pervasive and multitracked. It helped to nudge first the moral, then the social imaginary in the direction of modern individualism. This is what we see emerging in the new conception of moral order of seventeenth-century natural law theory. This was heavily indebted to Stoicism, and its originators were arguably the Netherlands neo-Stoics, Justus Lipsius and Hugo Grotius. But this was a Christianized Stoicism, and a modern one, in the sense that it gave a crucial place to a willed remaking of human society.

We could say that both the buffered identity and the project of reform contributed to the disembedding. Embeddedness, as I said above, is both a matter of identity—the contextual limits to the imagination of the self—and of the social imaginary: the ways we are able to think or imagine the whole of society. But the new buffered identity, with its insistence on personal devotion and discipline, increased the distance, the disidentification, even the hostility to the older forms of collective ritual and belonging, and the drive to reform came to envisage their abolition. Both in their sense of self and in their project for society, the disciplined elites moved toward a conception of the social world as constituted by individuals.

There is a problem with this kind of broad-gauge historical interpretation, which has already been recognized in the discussion of Weber's thesis about the development of the Protestant ethic and its relation to capitalism. Indeed, this is close to what I am saying here; it is a kind of specification of the broader connection I am asserting. Weber is obviously one of my sources.

An objection to Weber's thesis is that it can't be verified in terms of clearly traceable correlations between, say, confessional allegiances and capitalist development. But it is in the nature of this kind of relation between spiritual outlook and economic and political performance that the influence may also be much more diffuse and indirect. If we really believed, following the most vulgar forms of Marxism, that all change can be explained by nonspiritual factors, say in terms of economic motives, so that spiritual changes were always dependent variables, this wouldn't matter. But in fact, as I argued in chapter 3, the relationship is much more intimate and reciprocal. Certain moral self-understandings are embedded in certain practices, which can mean both that they are promoted by the spread of these practices and that they shape the practices and help them get established. It is equally absurd to believe that the practices always come first, or to adopt the opposite view, that ideas somehow drive history.

But this doesn't stop us from making sensible judgments about the relation of certain social forms and certain spiritual traditions. If Anglo-Saxon forms of capitalist entrepreneurship are much less connected to family relations than, say, Chinese forms, which seems undeniable,[14] has this really nothing to do with the difference between the Protestant conceptions of individual church membership versus the Confucian centrality of the family? This seems hard to credit, even if the microlinks can't all be traced.

Similarly, my thesis tries to link the undoubted primacy of the individual in modern Western culture, which is a central feature of the modern conception of moral order, to the earlier radical attempts to transform society along the principles of axial spirituality, tracing, in other words, how our present self-understandings grew.

It might easily seem that we don't need to trace this kind of genealogy because of the hold of subtraction stories. These are strong, because individualism has come to seem to us just common sense. The mistake of moderns is to take this understanding of the individual so much for granted that it is taken to be our first-off self-understanding "naturally." Just as, in modern epistemological thinking, a neutral description of things is thought to impinge first on us, and then values are added, so here we seize ourselves first as individuals, then become aware of others and of forms of sociality. This makes it easy to understand the emergence of modern individualism by a kind of subtraction story: the old horizons were eroded, burned away, and what emerges is the underlying sense of ourselves as individuals.

On the contrary, what I propose here is the idea that our first self-understanding was deeply embedded in society. Our essential identity was as father, son, and so on, and as a member of this tribe. Only later did we come to conceive of ourselves as free individuals first. This was not just a revolution in our neutral view of ourselves, but involved a profound change in our moral world, as is always the case with identity shifts.

This means that here too we have to distinguish between a formal and a material mode of social embedding, corresponding to the first two facets described above. On the first level, we are always socially embedded; we learn our identities in dialogue, by being inducted into a certain language. But on the level of content, what we may learn is to be an individual, have our own opinions, attain our own relation to God, our own conversion experience.

So the Great Disembedding occurs as a revolution in our understanding of moral-social order. And it goes on being accompanied by ideas of moral order. To be an individual is not to be a Robinson Crusoe, but to be placed in a certain way among other humans. This is the reflection of the transcendental necessity of holism just mentioned.

This disembeds us from the cosmic sacred—altogether, and not just partially and for certain people, as in earlier postaxial moves. It disembeds us from the social sacred and posits a new relation to God as designer. This new relation is eclipsable, because the design underlying the moral order can be seen as directed to ordinary human flourishing. This transcendent aspect of the axial revolution is partly rolled back, or can be, given a neat separation of this-worldly from otherworldly good. But only partly, because notions of flourishing remain under surveillance in our modern moral view: they have to fit with the demands of the moral order itself, of justice, equality, nondomination, if they are to escape condemnation. Our notions of flourishing can thus always be revised. This belongs to our postaxial condition.

This final phase of the Great Disembedding was largely powered by Christianity. But it was also in a sense a "corruption" of it, in Ivan Ilich's memorable phrase.[15] Powered by it, because the Gospel also is a disembedding. I mentioned above the calls to break away from the established solidarities. But this demand is present even more strongly in a parable like that of the Good Samaritan, as Ilich explains. It is not said, but inescapably implied. If the Samaritan had followed the demands of sacred social boundaries, he would never have stopped to help the wounded Jew. It is plain that the Kingdom involves another kind of solidarity altogether, one that would bring us into a network of agapê.

Here's where the corruption comes in: what we got was not a network of agapê, but rather a disciplined society in which

categorial relations have primacy and therefore norms. Nevertheless, it all started with the laudable attempt to fight back the demands of the world and then make it over. "World" (cosmos) in the New Testament has on the one hand a positive meaning, as in "God so loved the world" (John 3.16) and on the other a negative one: judge not as the world judges. This latter sense of world can be understood as the present sacralized order of things and its embedding in the cosmos.[16] In this sense, the church is rightly at odds with the world. This is what Hildebrand clearly saw when he fought to keep episcopal appointments out of the invasive power field of dynastic drive and ambition in the Investiture Controversy.

It might have seemed obvious that one should build on this defensive victory with an attempt to change and purify the power field of the world, make it more and more consonant with the demands of Christian spirituality. But this naturally didn't happen all at once. The changes were incremental, but the project was somehow continually reignited in more radical forms, through the various Reformations and down to the present age. The irony is that it somehow turned into something quite different; in another, rather different sense, the world won after all. Perhaps the contradiction lay in the very idea of a disciplined imposition of the Kingdom of God. The temptation of power was, after all, too strong, as Dostoyevsky saw in the legend of the Grand Inquisitor. Here lay the corruption.

Let us turn now to the way that the Great Disembedding has worked out in our modern social imaginary.

5 The Economy as Objectified Reality

There are in fact three important forms of social self-understanding which are crucial to modernity, and each of them represents a penetration or transformation of the social imaginary by the Grotian-Lockean theory of moral order. They are respectively the economy, the public sphere, and the practices and outlooks of democratic self-rule.

The economy was obviously linked with the self-understanding of polite civilization as grounded in a commercial society. But we can find the roots of this understanding further back, in the Grotian-Lockean idea of order itself.

I mentioned above that this new notion of order brought about a change in the understanding of the cosmos as the work of God's providence. We have here in fact one of the earliest examples of the new model of order moving beyond its original niche and reshaping the image of God's providential rule.

The notion that God governs the world according to a benign plan is ancient, even pre-Christian, with roots in Judaism as well as Stoicism. What is new is the way of conceiving of his benevolent scheme. We can see this in the arguments from the design of the world to the existence of a good Creator God. These too were very old. But formerly, they insisted on the magnificent design of the whole framework in which our world was set (the stars, the planets, etc.), and then on the admirable microdesign of creatures, including ourselves, with our organs fitted for their functions, as well as on the general way life was sustained by the processes of nature.

These conceptions certainly persist, but what is added in the eighteenth century is an appreciation of the way human life is designed to produce mutual benefit. Emphasis is sometimes laid on mutual benevolence, but very often the happy design is identified in the existence of what one might call "invisible hand" factors. I mean by this actions and attitudes that we are "programmed" for, that have systematically beneficent results for the general happiness, even though these are not part of what is intended in the action or affirmed in the attitude. Adam Smith in his *Wealth of Nations* provided us with the most famous of these mechanisms, whereby our search for our own individual prosperity redounds to the general welfare. But there are other examples, for instance, one drawn from his *Theory of Moral Sentiments*, where Smith argues that Nature has made us admire greatly rank and fortune because social order is much more secure if it rests on the respect for visible distinctions rather than on the less striking qualities of virtue and wisdom.[1]

The order here is that of a good engineering design, in which efficient causation plays the crucial role. In this it differs from earlier notions of order, where the harmony comes from the consonance among the Ideas or Forms manifested in the different levels of being or ranks in society. The crucial thing in the new conception is that our purposes mesh, however divergent they may be in the conscious awareness of each of us. They involve us in an exchange of advantages. We admire and support the rich and well-born, and in return we enjoy the kind of stable order without which prosperity would be impossible. God's design is one of interlocking causes, not of harmonized meanings.

In other words, humans are engaged in an exchange of services. The fundamental model seems to be what we have come to call an economy.

This new understanding of providence is already evident in Locke's formulation of natural law theory in the *Second Treatise*. We can see here how much importance the economic dimension is taking on in the new notion of order. There are two facets to this. The two main goals of organized society were security and economic prosperity, but because the whole theory emphasized a kind of profitable exchange, one could begin to see political society itself through a quasi-economic metaphor.

Thus, no less a personage than Louis XIV, in the advice he offers to his dauphin, subscribes to something like an exchange view: "All these different conditions that compose the world are united to each other only by an exchange of reciprocal obligations. The deference and respect that we receive from our subjects are not a free gift from them but payment for the justice and protection they expect to receive from us."[2]

This, incidentally, offers some insight into (what turned out to be) an important transitional stage on the long march of the order of mutual benefit into our social imaginary. This was a rival model of order based on command and hierarchy. What Louis and others of his time were offering can be seen as a kind of compromise between the new and the old. The basic justifying reasoning of the different functions, here ruler and subject, is new: the necessary and fruitful exchange of services. But what is justified is still a hierarchical society and, above all, the most radical hierarchical relation, that of absolute monarch to subject. The justification is more and more in terms of functional necessity, but the master images still reflect something of inherent superiority, an ontological hierarchy. The king, by being above everyone else, can hold society together and sustain everything. He is like the sun, to use Louis's favorite image.[3]

We might call this the Baroque solution,[4] except that its most spectacular example, at Versailles, saw itself in Classical terms. It is this compromise that reigns for a while over most of Europe, sustaining regimes with much of the pomp, ritual, and imagery of hierarchical complementarity, but on the basis of a justification drawn more and more from the modern order. Bossuet's defense of Louis's absolute rule falls in the same register.

But the economy could become more than a metaphor: it came to be seen more and more as the dominant end of society. Contemporary with Louis's memoir of advice, Montchrétien offers a theory of the state that sees it as primarily the orchestrating power that can make an economy flourish. (It is he, incidentally, who seems to have coined the term "political economy.") Merchants act for love of gain, but good policy by the ruler (here, a very visible hand) can draw this love to the common good.[5]

This second shift reflects feature (2) of the modern order in my sketch in chapter 1: the mutual benefit we are meant to confer on each other gives a crucial place to the securing of life and the means to life. This is not an isolated change within theories of providence; it goes along with a major trend of the age.

This trend is often understood in terms of the standard materialist explanations, which I evoked in chapter 3, for instance, the old Marxist account that business classes, merchants, and later manufacturers were becoming more numerous and gaining greater power. Even on its own level, this account needs to be supplemented with a reference to the changing demands of state power. It more and more dawned on governing elites that increased production and favorable exchange were key conditions of political and military power. The experiences of Holland and England demonstrated that. And, of course, once some nations began to develop economically, their rivals were forced to follow suit or be relegated to dependent status. This, as much as if not more than the growing numbers and wealth, was responsible for the enhanced position of commercial classes.

These factors were important, but they cannot provide the whole explanation of the change in self-understanding. What started us on this path were changes on several levels, not only economic, but political and spiritual. In this I think Weber is right, even if not all the details of his theory can be salvaged.

The original importance of people working steadily in a profession came from the fact that they thereby placed themselves in "settled courses," to use the Puritan expression. If ordered life became a demand, not just for a military or spiritual/intellectual elite but for the mass of ordinary people, then everyone had to become ordered and serious about what they were doing, and of necessity had to be doing, in life, namely, working in some productive occupation. A truly ordered society requires that one take these economic occupations seriously and prescribe a discipline for them. This was the political ground.

But in Reformed Christianity, and to a growing extent among Catholics as well, there was a pressing spiritual reason to make this demand, which was the one Weber picked up on. To put it in the Reformed variant: if we are going to reject the Catholic idea that there are some higher vocations, to the celibate or monastic life, following "counsels of perfection," and if one claims that all Christians must be 100 percent Christian and that one can be so in any vocation, then one must claim that ordinary life, the life that the vast majority cannot help leading, the life of production and the family, work and sex, is as hallowed as any other. Indeed, more so than monastic celibacy, because that is based on the vain and prideful claim to have found a higher way.

This is the basis for that sanctification of ordinary life, which I claim has had a tremendous formative effect on Western civilization, spilling beyond the original religious variant into myriad secular forms. It has two facets: it promotes ordinary life as a site for the highest forms of Christian life, and it also has an anti-elitist thrust: it takes down those allegedly higher modes of existence, whether in the Church (monastic vocations) or in the world (ancient-derived ethics that place contemplation higher than productive existence). The mighty are cast down from their seats and the humble and meek are exalted.

Both these facets have been formative in the development of modern civilization. The affirmation of ordinary life is part of the background to the central place given to the economic in our lives, as also for the tremendous importance we put on family life, or relationships. The anti-elitist position underlies the fundamental importance of equality in our social and political lives.[6]

All these factors, material and spiritual, help explain the gradual promotion of the economic to its central place, a promotion already clearly visible in the eighteenth century. At that time, another factor enters, or perhaps it is simply an extension of the political factor. The notion becomes more and more accredited that commerce and economic activity are the path to peace and orderly existence. "Le doux commerce" is contrasted to the wild destructiveness of the aristocratic search for military glory. The more a society turns to commerce, the more polished and civilized it becomes, the more it excels in the arts of peace. The impetus to moneymaking is seen as a "calm passion." When it takes hold in a society, it can help to control and inhibit the violent passions. Put in other language, moneymaking serves our interest, and interest can check and control passion.[7] Kant even believed that as nations become republics, and hence more under the control of their ordinary taxpayers actuated by economic interests, recourse to war will become rarer and rarer.

The new economically centered notion of natural order underlies the doctrines of harmony of interest. It even came to be projected onto the universe, for it is this that is reflected in the eighteenth-century vision of cosmic order, not as a hierarchy of forms-at-work, but as a chain of beings whose purposes mesh with each other. Things cohere because they serve each other in their survival and flourishing. They form an ideal economy.

> See dying vegetables life sustain,
> See life dissolving vegetate again:
> All forms that perish other forms supply,
> (By turns we catch the vital breath, and die)
> Like bubbles on the sea of Matter born,
> They rise, they break, and to that sea return.
> Nothing is foreign: Parts relate to whole;
> One all-extending, all preserving Soul
>
> Connects each being, greatest with the least;
> Made Beast in aid of Man, and Man of Beast;
> All served, all serving: nothing stands alone;
> The chain holds on, and where it ends, unknown.
> . . . .
> God in nature of each being founds
> Its proper bliss, and sets its proper bounds;
> But as he framed a Whole, the Whole to bless,
> On mutual Wants built mutual Happiness:
> So from the first, eternal ORDER ran,
> And creature linked to creature, man to man.

From all this, Pope triumphantly concludes "that true SELF-LOVE and SOCIAL are the same."[8]

And so perhaps the first big shift wrought by this new idea of order, both in theory and in social imaginary, consists in our coming to see our society as an economy, an interlocking set of activities of production, exchange, and consumption, which form a system with its own laws and its own dynamic. Instead of being merely the management, by those in authority, of the resources we collectively need in household or state, the economic now defines a way we are linked together, a sphere of coexistence that in principle could suffice to itself, if only disorder and conflict didn't threaten. Conceiving of the economy as a system is an achievement of eighteenth-century theory, with the physiocrats and Adam Smith, but coming to see the most important purpose and agenda of society as economic collaboration and exchange is a drift in our social imaginary that begins in that period and continues to this day. From that point on, organized society is no longer equivalent to the polity; other dimensions of social existence are seen as having their own forms and integrity. The very shift in this period of the meaning of the term civil society reflects this.

This is the first of the three forms of social imaginary I want to discuss. But before passing to the second, I want to bring out a general feature of our modern self-understanding which comes to light when we contrast the economy with the other two forms. Both of these—the public sphere and the self-ruling "people"—imagine us as collective agencies. And it is these new modes of collective agency that are among the most striking features of Western modernity and beyond; we understand ourselves after all to be living in a democratic age.

But the account of economic life in terms of an invisible hand is quite different. There is no collective agent here; indeed, the account amounts to a denial of such. There are agents, individuals acting on their own behalf, but the global upshot happens behind their backs. It has a certain predictable form, because there are certain laws governing the way in which their myriad individual actions concatenate.

This is an objectifying account, one that treats social events like other processes in nature, as following laws of a similar sort. But this objectifying take on social life is just as much a part of the modern understanding, derived from the modern moral order, as the new modes of imagining social agency. The two belong together as parts of the same package. Once we are no longer dealing with an idea of social order as Forms-at-work in reality, of the kind invoked by Plato, but as forms imposed on inert reality by human agency, we need pictures of the layout of this inert reality and the causal connections that structure it, just as much as we need models of our collective action on it. The engineer needs to know the laws of the domain in which he is going to work, just as much as he needs a plan of what he is trying to achieve; indeed, the second can't be drawn up unless the first is known.

And so this age also sees the beginnings of a new kind of objectifying social science, starting with William Petty's survey in Ireland in the mid-seventeenth century, the collection of facts and statistics about wealth, production, and demography as the basis for policy. Objectifying pictures of social reality are just as prominent a feature of Western modernity as the constitution of large-scale collective agencies.[9] The modern grasp of society is ineradicably bifocal.

To better understand this change in the nature of science, we should see it from the other side of the divide. As long as society was understood in terms of something resembling a Platonic- or Aristotelian-type teleology, this kind of bifocal take was not possible. In speaking of teleology, I don't want to invoke any heavy metaphysical doctrines; I am talking of a widespread understanding of society as having a "normal" order, which tended to maintain itself over time but could be threatened by certain developments, which, taken beyond a certain point, could precipitate a slide toward destruction, civil strife, or the utter loss of the proper form. We can see this as an understanding of society very analogous to our understanding ourselves as organisms in terms of the key concepts of health and sickness.

Even Machiavelli still has an understanding of this kind when it comes to republican forms. There is a certain equilibrium-in-tension that needs to be maintained between the *grandi* and the people if these forms are to survive. In healthy polities, this equilibrium is maintained by the play or rivalry and mutual surveillance between the orders. But certain developments threaten this, such as an excessive interest on the part of citizens in their private wealth and property. This constitutes *corruzione*, and unless dealt with in time, and severely, will bring about the end of republican liberty. There is a causal attribution here: wealth undermines liberty. But the term "corruption," with its strong normative resonances, shows that the understanding of society is being organized around a concept of normal form.

As long as social thought is organized in this way, the bifocal take can't get a hold. Reality is not understood as inert, but as shaped by a normal form, which maintains itself within certain limits of distance from its proper shape, and beyond them spirals off to destruction, just as the healthy human body does. Successful collective action is seen as taking place within a field shaped by this form; indeed, this form is its condition. Once we lose it, collective action disintegrates into the corrupt strivings of self-regarding individuals. There is neither inert reality, nor action ab extra imposing some shape on this reality.

One might think that the Smithian notion of an invisible hand defines a new "normal" order, one of mutual enrichment; in some ways, it can be treated as such, and is so invoked by various neoliberal boosters of the market in our day. But it is not an order of collective action, for the market is the negation of collective action. To operate properly, it requires a certain pattern of interventions (keeping order, enforcing contracts, setting weights and measures, etc.) and (tirelessly stressed) noninterventions (get the government off our backs). But what is striking about the Smithian invisible hand, from the standpoint of the old science, is that it is a spontaneous order arising among *corrupt*, that is, purely self-regarding actors. It is not a finding that, like Machiavelli's link between wealth and corruption, pertains to the normative conditions of proper collective action.

In a science concerned with these conditions, there is room neither for action unenframed by a normatively constituted reality, nor for a study of a normatively neutral, inert social field. Neither component of the modern bifocal take can find a niche.

This shift in the nature of science is also connected to the change I noted a few paragraphs back. For moderns, organized society is no longer equivalent to the polity. Once we discover the impersonal processes happening behind the backs of agents, there may well be other aspects of society that show some law-like systematicity. The invisible-hand–guided economy is one such aspect; other facets of social life or culture or demography will later be singled out for scientific treatment. There will be more than one way in which the same body of systematically interacting human beings can be considered as forming an entity, a society. We can speak of them as an economy or a state or a civil society (now identified in its nonpolitical aspects) or just as a society or a culture. "Society" has been unhooked from "polity" and now floats free through a number of different applications.

Much in this scientific revolution turns on the rejection of a mode of normative thinking in terms of telê. This rejection was also a central part of much of the moral thinking that emerges from the modern idea of order, which found expression in the anti-Aristotelian animus of Locke and those he influenced. Of course, the rejection of teleology was famously motivated by a stance supporting the new, mechanistic science. But it was also animated by the emerging moral theory. What distinguished the new, atomist, natural law theory from its predecessor as formulated by Aquinas, for instance, was its thoroughgoing detachment from the Aristotelian matrix which had been central for Thomas. The correct political forms were not deducible from a telos at work in human society. What justified the law was either its being commanded by God (Locke), or its making logical sense, given the rational and social nature of humans (Grotius), or (later) its providing a way of securing the harmony of interests.[10]

The modern bifocal take is not without its tensions. I mentioned earlier that freedom as a central good is overdetermined in the modern moral order: it is both one of the central properties of the humans who consent to and thus constitute society, and it is inscribed in their condition as the artificers who build their own social world, as against being born into one that already has its own normal form. Indeed, one of the reasons for the vigorous rejection of Aristotelian teleology was that it was seen, then as now, as potentially circumscribing our freedom to determine our own lives and build our own societies.

But just for this reason, a battle could break out between the two takes. What for one school falls into the domain of an objective take on unavoidable reality may seem to another to be a surrender of the human capacity to design our world before a false positivity. The very importance given to freedom is bound to give rise to this kind of challenge. This sort of critique has been central to the work of Rousseau, and beyond him to Fichte, Hegel, and Marx. We don't need to underline the importance they have had in our civilization. The ambition to transform what is lived just *an sich* into something assumed *für sich*, to use the Hegel-Marx terminology, is ever-recurring. We see this in the constant attempt to transform what are at first merely objective sociological categories (e.g., handicapped, welfare recipients) into collective agencies through mobilizing movements.

But before these philosophers wrote, and influencing their work, was the civic humanist tradition, the ethic of republican self-rule. Here we come to a tension that has been inseparable from the modern moral order itself. Even while it has advanced and colonized our modern social imaginaries, it has awakened unease and suspicion. We saw that its entrenchment was connected to the self-understanding of modern society as commercial, and that the transition to the commercial stage was understood as having effected the great internal pacification of modern states. This society dethroned war as the highest human activity and put in its place production. It was hostile to the older codes of warrior honor, and it tended toward a certain leveling.

All this could not but provoke resistance. This came not just from the orders that had a stake in the old way of things, the noblesse de l'épée; many people from all stations were ambivalent about it. With the coming of a commercial society, it seemed that greatness, heroism, and full-hearted dedication to a nonutilitarian cause were in danger of atrophy, even of disappearing from the world.

One form this worry took was the concern about men, following the ethos of polite society, becoming "effeminate," losing their manly virtues, which was an important recurring theme in the eighteenth century. At the most primitive level, this could emerge in a rebellion of upper-class rowdies against the polite conventions of the age; at a slightly higher level perhaps, in the return of duelling in eighteenth-century England.[11] But at the highest level, it promoted the ethic of civic humanism as a rival to the ethos of commercial society, or perhaps as a compensation for the dangers—of enervation, corruption, loss of liberty—that this modern form brought with it. This was not a marginal concern; it occupied some of the most influential thinkers of the age, such as Adam Smith.[12]

These worries and tensions have remained a central part of modern culture. In one form, they could lead to a transformed redaction of the modern idea of order—to save civic virtue or freedom or nonalienated self-rule, as we find in the philosophies of Rousseau and Marx. In another, they were indeed seen as a potential threat of degeneracy inherent in the order, but by people who in no way wanted to reject this order merely to find some prophylactic for its dangerous potentialities. Smith, and later Tocqueville, belong to this category.

The concern about leveling, the end of heroism, of greatness, has also been turned into a fierce denunciation of the modern moral order and everything it stands for, as we see with Nietzsche. Attempts to build a polity around a rival notion of order in the very heart of modern civilization, most notably the various forms of fascism and related authoritarianism, have failed. But the continued popularity of Nietzsche shows that his devastating critique still speaks to many people today. The modern order, though entrenched, perhaps even because entrenched, still awakens much resistance.

6   The Public Sphere

The economic was perhaps the first dimension of civil society to achieve an identity independent from the polity. But it was followed shortly afterward by the public sphere.

The public sphere is a common space in which the members of society are deemed to meet through a variety of media: print, electronic, and also face-to-face encounters; to discuss matters of common interest; and thus to be able to form a common mind about these. I say "*a* common space" because although the media are multiple, as are the exchanges that take place in them, they are deemed to be in principle intercommunicating. The discussion we're having on television now takes account of what was said in the newspaper this morning, which in turn reports on the radio debate yesterday, and so on. That's why we usually speak of the public sphere in the singular.

The public sphere is a central feature of modern society, so much so that even where it is in fact suppressed or manipulated it has to be faked. Modern despotic societies have generally felt compelled to go through the motions. Editorials in the party newspapers, purporting to express the opinions of the writers, are offered for the consideration of their fellow citizens; mass demonstrations are organized, purporting to give vent to the felt indignation of large numbers of people. All this takes place as though a genuine process were in train, forming a common mind through exchange, even though the result is carefully controlled from the beginning.

In this discussion, I draw in particular on two very interesting books. One was published almost thirty years ago but recently translated into English, Jürgen Habermas's *The Structural Transformation of the Public Sphere*, which deals with the development of public opinion in eighteenth-century Western Europe; the other is a recent publication by Michael Warner, *The Letters of the Republic*, which describes the analogous phenomenon in the British American colonies.[1]

A central theme of Habermas's book is the emergence in Western Europe in the eighteenth century of a new concept of public opinion. Dispersed publications and small group or local exchanges come to be construed as one big debate, from which the public opinion of a whole society emerges. In other words, it is understood that widely separated people sharing the same view have been linked in a kind of space of discussion, wherein they have been able to exchange ideas with others and reach this common end point.

What is this common space? It's a rather strange thing, when one comes to think of it. The people involved here have, by hypothesis, never met but they are seen as linked in a common space of discussion through media—in the eighteenth century, print media. Books, pamphlets, and newspapers circulated among the educated public, conveying theses, analyses, arguments, and counterarguments, referring to and refuting each other. These were widely read and often discussed in face-to-face gatherings, in drawing rooms, coffeehouses, salons, and in more (authoritatively) public places, like Parliament. The general view that resulted from all this, if any, counted as public opinion in this new sense.

This space is a public sphere in the sense I'm using it here. That a conclusion "counts as" public opinion reflects the fact that a public sphere can exist only if it is imagined as such. Unless all the dispersed discussions are seen by their participants as linked in one great exchange, there can be no sense of their upshot as public opinion. This doesn't mean that imagination is all-powerful. There are objective conditions: internal, for instance, that the fragmentary local discussions interrefer; and external, that is, there must be printed materials, circulating from a plurality of independent sources, for there to be bases of what can be seen as a common discussion. As is often said, the modern public sphere relied on "print capitalism" to get going. But as Warner shows, printing itself, and even print capitalism, didn't provide a sufficient condition. They had to be taken up in the right cultural context, where the essential common understandings could arise.[2] The public sphere was a mutation of the social imaginary, one crucial to the development of modern society. It was an important step on the long march.

We are now in a slightly better position to understand what kind of thing a public sphere is, and why it was new in the eighteenth century. It's a kind of common space, I have been saying, in which people who never meet understand themselves to be engaged in discussion and capable of reaching a common mind. Let me introduce some new terminology. We can speak of common space when people come together in a common act of focus for whatever purpose, be it ritual, the enjoyment of a play, conversation, or the celebration of a major event. Their focus is common, as against merely convergent, because it is part of what is commonly understood that they are attending to, the common object or purpose, together, as against each person just happening, on his or her own, to be concerned with the same thing. In this sense, the "opinion of mankind" offers a merely convergent unity, whereas public opinion is supposedly generated out of a series of common actions.

An intuitively understandable kind of common space is set up when people are assembled for some purpose, be it on an intimate level for conversation or on a larger, more public scale for a deliberative assembly, a ritual, a celebration, or the enjoyment of a football match or an opera. Common space arising from assembly in some locale is what I want to call "topical common space."

But the public sphere is something different. It transcends such topical spaces. We might say that it knits together a plurality of such spaces into one larger space of nonassembly. The same public discussion is deemed to pass through our debate today, and someone else's earnest conversation tomorrow, and the newspaper interview Thursday, and so on. I call this larger kind of nonlocal common space "metatopical." The public sphere that emerges in the eighteenth century is a metatopical common space.

Such spaces are partly constituted by common understandings; that is, they are not reducible to but cannot exist without such understandings. New, unprecedented kinds of spaces require new and unprecedented understandings. Such is the case for the public sphere.

What is new is not metatopicality. The Church and the state were already existing metatopical spaces. But getting clear about the novelty brings us to the essential features of the public sphere as a step in the long march.

I see it as a step in this march because this mutation in the social imaginary was inspired by the modern idea of order. Two features stand out in this regard. One has just been implied: its independent identity from the political. The other is its force as a benchmark of legitimacy. Why these are important will be clear if we recur to the original idealization, say, with Grotius or Locke.

First, in the Grotius-Locke idealization political society is seen as an instrument for something prepolitical; there is a place to stand, mentally, outside of the polity, as it were, from which to judge its performance. This is what is reflected in the new ways of imagining social life independent of the political, namely, the economy and the public sphere.

Second, freedom is central to the rights society exists to defend. Responding both to this and to the underlying notion of agency, the theory puts great importance on the requirement that political society be founded on the consent of those bound by it.

Now contract theories of legitimate government had existed before. What is new in the theories of the seventeenth century is that they put the requirement of consent at a more fundamental level. It was not just that a people, conceived as already existing, had to give consent to those who would claim to rule it. Now the original contract brings us out of the state of nature and even founds the existence of a collectivity that has some claim on its member individuals.

This original demand for once-for-all historical consent as a condition of legitimacy can easily develop into a requirement of current consent. Government must win the consent of the governed — not just originally, but as an ongoing condition of legitimacy. This is what begins to surface in the legitimation function of public opinion.

These features of the public sphere can be clarified by articulating what is new about it on two levels: what the public sphere *does*; and what it *is*.

First, what it does, or rather, what is done in it. The public sphere is the locus of a discussion potentially engaging everyone (although, in the eighteenth century, the claim was only to involve the educated or "enlightened" minority), in which the society can come to a common mind about important matters. This common mind is a reflective view, emerging from critical debate, and not just a summation of whatever views happen to be held in the population.³ As a consequence, it has a normative status: government ought to listen to it. There were two reasons for this, of which one tended to gain ground and ultimately swallow up the other. The first is that this opinion is likely to be enlightened, and hence government would be well-advised to follow it. This statement by Louis Sébastien Mercier, quoted by Habermas,⁴ gives clear expression to this idea:

> Les bons livres dépendent des lumières dans toutes les classes du peuple; ils ornent la vérité. Ce sont eux qui déjà gouvernent l'Europe; ils éclairent le gouvernement sur ses devoirs, sur sa faute, sur son véritable intérêt, sur l'opinion publique qu'il doit écouter et suivre: ces bons livres sont des maîtres patients qui attendent le réveil des administrateurs des États et le calme de leurs passions.

> (Good books depend on enlightenment in all classes of the people; they adorn the truth. It is they who already govern Europe; they enlighten the government about its duties, its errors, its real interest, the public opinion that it should listen to and follow: these good books are patient masters who await the awakening of those who administer states and the calming of their passions.)

Kant famously had a similar view.

The second reason emerges with the view that the people are sovereign. Government is then not only wise to follow opinion; it is morally bound to do so. Governments ought to legislate and rule in the midst of a reasoning public. In making its decisions, Parliament or the court ought to be concentrating together and enacting what has already been emerging out of enlightened debate among the people. From this arises what Warner, following Habermas, calls the "principle of supervision," which insists that the proceedings of governing bodies be public, open to the scrutiny of discerning citizens.[5] By going public, legislative deliberation informs public opinion and allows it to be maximally rational, at the same time exposing itself to its pressure and thus acknowledging that legislation should ultimately bow to the clear mandates of this opinion.[6]

The public sphere is, then, a locus in which rational views are elaborated that should guide government. This comes to be seen as an essential feature of a free society. As Burke put it, "In a free country, every man thinks he has a concern in all public matters".[7] There is, of course, something very new about this in the eighteenth century compared to the immediate past of Europe. But one might ask, is this new in history? Isn't this a feature of all free societies?

89

No, there is a subtle but important difference. Let's compare the modern society with a public sphere with an ancient republic or polis. In the latter, we can imagine that debate on public affairs may be carried on in a host of settings: among friends at a symposium, between those who meet in the agora, and then of course in the ekklesia, where the thing is finally decided. The debate swirls around and ultimately reaches its conclusion in the competent decision-making body. The difference is that the discussions outside this body prepare for the action ultimately taken by the same people within it. The "unofficial" discussions are not separated off, given a status of their own, and seen to constitute a kind of metatopical space.

But that is what happens with the modern public sphere. It is a space of discussion that is self-consciously seen as being outside power. It is supposed to be listened to by power, but it is not itself an exercise of power. Its in this sense extrapolitical status is crucial. As we shall see below, it links the public sphere with other facets of modern society that are also seen as essentially extrapolitical. The extrapolitical status is not just defined negatively, as a lack of power. It is also seen positively: because public opinion is not an exercise of power, it can be ideally disengaged from partisan spirit and rational.

In other words, with the modern public sphere comes the idea that political power must be supervised and checked by something outside. What was new, of course, was not that there was an outside check, but rather the nature of this instance. It is not defined as the will of God or the law of Nature (although it could be thought to articulate these), but as a kind of discourse, emanating from reason and not from power or traditional authority. As Habermas puts it, power was to be tamed by reason: "veritas non auctoritas facit legem."[8]

In this way, the public sphere was different from everything preceding it. An unofficial discussion, which nevertheless can come to a verdict of great importance, is defined outside the sphere of power. It borrows some of the images from ancient assemblies (this was especially prominent in the American case) to project the whole public as one space of discussion. But, as Warner shows, it innovates in relation to this model. Those who intervene are like speakers before an assembly. But unlike their models in real ancient assemblies, they strive for a certain impersonality, a certain impartiality, an eschewing of party spirit. They strive to negate their own particularity and thus to rise above "any private or partial view." This is what Warner calls "the principle of negativity." We can see it not only as suiting with the print, as against spoken, medium, but also as giving expression to this crucial feature of the new public sphere as extrapolitical, as a discourse of reason *on* and *to* power rather than *by* power.[9]

As Warner points out, the rise of the public sphere involves a breach in the old ideal of a social order undivided by conflict and difference. On the contrary, it means that debate breaks out, and continues, involving in principle everybody, and this is perfectly legitimate. The old unity will be gone forever, but a new unity is to be substituted. For the ever-continuing controversy is not meant to be an exercise in power, a quasi–civil war carried on by dialectical means. Its potentially divisive and destructive consequences are offset by the fact that it is a debate outside of power, a rational debate, striving without parti pris to define the common good. "The language of resistance to controversy articulates a norm for controversy. It silently transforms the ideal of a social order free from conflictual debate into an ideal of debate free from social conflict."[10]

So what the public sphere does is enable the society to come to a common mind, without the mediation of the political sphere, in a discourse of reason outside power, which nevertheless is normative for power. Now let's try to see what, in order to do this, it has to *be*.

We can perhaps best do this by trying to define what is new and unprecedented in it. And I want to get to this in two steps, as it were. First, there is the aspect of its novelty which has already been touched on. When we compare the public sphere with one of the important sources of its constitutive images, viz., the ancient republic, what springs to our notice is its extrapolitical locus. The "Republic of Letters" was a common term that members of the international society of savants in interchange gave themselves toward the end of the seventeenth century. This was a precursor phenomenon to the public sphere; indeed, it contributed to shaping it. Here was a "republic" constituted outside of the political.

Both the analogy and the difference gave its force and point to this image: it was a republic as a unified association, grouping all enlightened participants across political boundaries. But it was also a republic in being free from subjection; its "citizens" owed no allegiance but to it as long as they went about the business of Letters.

Something of this is inherited by the eighteenth-century public sphere. Within it, members of society come together and pursue a common end; they form and understand themselves to form an association, which is nevertheless not constituted by its political structure. This was not true of the ancient polis or republic. Athens was a society, a *koinônia*, only as constituted politically. The same was true of Rome. The ancient society was given its identity by its laws. On the banners of the legions, SPQR stood for "Senatus populusque romanus," but the "populus" here was the ensemble of Roman citizens, that is, those defined as such by the laws. The people didn't have an identity, didn't constitute a unity prior to and outside of these laws. This reflected, as we saw above, a common premodern understanding of the moral/metaphysical order underlying social practice.

By contrast, in projecting a public sphere, our eighteenth-century forebears were placing themselves in an association, this common space of discussion, which owed nothing to political structures but was seen as existing independently of them.

This extrapolitical status is one aspect of the newness of the public sphere: that all members of a political society (or at least, all the competent and enlightened members) should be seen as also forming a society outside the state. Indeed, this society was wider than any one state; it extended for some purposes to all of civilized Europe. This is an extremely important aspect, and corresponds to a crucial feature of our contemporary civilization, which emerges at this time and which is visible in more than the public sphere. I will take this up momentarily, but first we have to take the second step.

For it is obvious that an extrapolitical, international society is by itself not new. It is preceded by the Stoic cosmopolis, and, more immediately, by the Christian Church. Europeans were used to living in a dual society, one organized by two mutually irreducible principles. So the second facet of the newness of the public sphere has to be defined as its radical secularity.

Here I am recurring to a very particular use of this term, in which it stands close to its original meaning as an expression for a certain kind of time. It is obviously intimately related to one common meaning of secularity, which focuses on the removal of God or religion or the spiritual from public space. What I am talking about is not exactly that, but something that has contributed to it, namely, a shift in our understanding of what society is grounded on. In spite of all the risks of confusion, there is a reason to use the term secular here because it marks in its very etymology what is at stake in this context, which has something to do with the way human society inhabits time. But this way of describing the difference requires some preliminary exploration.

This notion of secularity is radical because it stands in contrast not only with a divine foundation for society, but with any idea of society as constituted in something that transcends contemporary common action. If we recur to the premodern ideas of order described in chapter 1, we find, for instance, hierarchical societies that conceive of themselves as bodying forth some part of the Chain of Being. Behind the empirical fillers of the slots of kingship, aristocracy, and so on lie the Ideas or the persisting metaphysical Realities that these people are momentarily embodying. The king has two bodies, only one being the particular, perishable one, which is now being fed and clothed and will later be buried.[11] Within this outlook, what constitutes a society as such is the metaphysical order it embodies.[12] People act within a framework that exists prior to and independent of their action.

But secularity contrasts not only with divinely established churches or Great Chains. It is also different from an understanding of our society as constituted by a law that has been ours since time out of mind. Because this, too, places our action within a framework, one that binds us together, makes us a society, and transcends our common action.

In contradistinction to all this, the public sphere is an association that is constituted by nothing outside of the common action we carry out in it: coming to a common mind, where possible, through the exchange of ideas. Its existence as an association is just our acting together in this way. This common action is not made possible by a framework that needs to be established in some action-transcendent dimension, either by an act of God or in a Great Chain or by a law that comes down to us since time out of mind. This is what makes it radically secular. And this gets us to the heart of what is new and unprecedented in it.

This is baldly stated. Obviously, this notion of secularity needs to be made still clearer. Perhaps the contrast is obvious enough with Mystical Bodies and Great Chains. But I am claiming a difference from traditional tribal society as well, the kind of thing the German peoples had who founded our modern North Atlantic polities, or in another form, what constituted the ancient republics and poleis. And this might be challenged.

These societies were defined by a law. But is that all that different from the public sphere? After all, whenever we want to act in this sphere, we meet a number of structures already in place: there are certain newspapers, television networks, publishing houses, and the rest. We act within the channels that these provide. Is this not rather analogous to any member of a tribe, who also has to act within established structures of chieftainships, councils, annual meetings, and the rest? Of course, the institutions of the public sphere change; newspapers go broke, television networks merge. But no tribe remains absolutely fixed in its forms; these too evolve over time. If one wanted to claim that this preexisting structure is valid for ongoing action, but not for the founding acts that set up the public sphere, the answer might be that these are impossible to identify in the stream of time, any more than they are for the tribe. And if we want to insist that there must be such a moment, then we should remark that many tribes as well hand down legends of a founding act, when a Lycurgus, for instance, laid down their laws. Surely he acted outside of existing structures.

Talking of actions within structures brings out the similarities. But there is an important difference that resides in the respective common understandings. It is true that in a functioning public sphere, action at any time is carried out within structures laid down earlier. There is a de facto arrangement of things. But this arrangement doesn't enjoy any privilege over the action carried out within it. The structures were set up during previous acts of communication in common space, on all fours with those we are carrying out now. Our present action may modify these structures, and that is perfectly legitimate, because these are seen as nothing more than precipitates and facilitators of such communicative action.

But the traditional law of a tribe usually enjoys a different status. We may, of course, alter it over time, following the prescription it itself provides. But it is not seen just as a precipitate and facilitator of action. The abolition of the law would mean the abolition of the subject of common action, because the law defines the tribe as an entity. Whereas a public sphere could start up again, even where all media had been abolished, simply by founding new ones, a tribe can resume its life only on the understanding that the law, although perhaps interrupted in its efficacy by foreign conquest, is still in force.

That's what I mean when I say that what constitutes the society, what makes the common agency possible, transcends the common actions carried out within it. It is not just that the structures we need for today's common action arose as a consequence of yesterday's, which, however, was no different in nature from today's. Rather, the traditional law is a precondition of any common action, at whatever time, because this common agency couldn't exist without it. It is in this sense transcendent. By contrast, in a purely secular association (in my sense), common agency arises simply in and as a precipitate of common action.

The crucial distinction underlying this concept of secularity can thus be related to this issue: What constitutes the association? Or otherwise put, What makes this group of people as they continue over time a common agent? Where this is something that transcends the realm of those common actions this agency engages in, the association is nonsecular. Where the constituting factor is nothing other than such common action—whether the founding acts have already occurred in the past or are now coming about is immaterial—we have secularity.

This kind of secularity is modern; it came about very recently in the history of mankind. Of course, there have been all sorts of momentary and topical common agents that have arisen just from common action. A crowd gathers, people shout protests, and then the governor's house is stoned or the chateau is burned down. But prior to the modern day, enduring, metatopical common agency was inconceivable on a purely secular basis. People could see themselves only as constituted into such by something action-transcendent, be it a foundation by God or a Chain of Being that society bodied forth or some traditional law that defined our people. The eighteenth-century public sphere thus represents an instance of a new kind: a metatopical common space and common agency without an action-transcendent constitution, an agency grounded purely in its own common actions.

But how about the founding moments traditional societies often "remembered"? What about Lycurgus's action in giving Sparta its laws? Surely these show us examples of the constituting factor (here law) issuing from common action: Lycurgus proposes, the Spartans accept. But it is in the nature of such founding moments that they are not put on the same plane as contemporary common action. The foundation acts are displaced onto a higher plane, into a heroic time, an *illud tempus* which is not seen as qualitatively on a level with what we do today. The founding action is not like our action, not just an earlier similar act whose precipitate structures ours. It is not just earlier, but in another kind of time, an exemplary time.[13]

This is why I am tempted to use the term secular in spite of all the misunderstandings that may arise. Because it's clear that I don't mean only "not tied to religion."[14] The exclusion is much broader. For the original sense of secular was "of the age," that is, pertaining to profane time. It was close to the sense of "temporal" in the opposition temporal/spiritual, as we saw earlier.

In earlier ages, the understanding was that this profane time existed in relation to (surrounded by, penetrated by; it is hard to find the right words here) higher times. Premodern understandings of time seem to have been always multidimensional. Time was transcended and held in place by eternity, whether that of Greek philosophy or of the biblical God. In either case, eternity was not just endless profane time, but an ascent into the unchanging, or a kind of gathering of time into a unity; hence the expression "hoi aiônes tôn aiônôn" or "saecula saeculorum" (through the ages of ages).

The Platonic or Christian relating of time and eternity were not the only games in town, even in Christendom. There was also the much more widespread sense of a foundation time, a "time of origins," as Eliade calls it,[15] which was complexly related to the present moment in ordinary time, in that it frequently could be ritually approached and its force partly reappropriated at certain privileged moments. That's why it could not simply be unambiguously placed in the past (in ordinary time). The Christian liturgical year draws on this kind of time consciousness, widely shared by other religions, in reenacting the "founding" events of Christ's life.

It seems to have been the universal norm to see the important metatopical spaces and agencies as constituted in some mode of higher time. States and churches were seen to exist almost necessarily in more than one time dimension, as though it were inconceivable that they have their being purely in the profane or ordinary time. A state that bodied forth the Great Chain was connected to the eternal realm of Ideas; a people defined by its law communicated with the founding time where this was laid down; and so on.

Modern secularization can be seen from one angle as the rejection of higher times and the positing of time as purely profane. Events now exist only in this one dimension, in which they stand at greater and lesser temporal distance and in relations of causality with other events of the same kind. The modern notion of simultaneity comes to be, in which events utterly unrelated in cause or meaning are held together simply by their co-occurrence at the same point in this single profane time line. Modern literature, as well as news media, seconded by social science, have accustomed us to think of society in terms of vertical time slices, holding together myriad happenings, related and unrelated. I think Benedict Anderson is right that this is a typically modern mode of social imagination, which our medieval forebears would have found difficult to understand, for where events in profane time are very differently related to higher time, it seems unnatural just to group them side by side in the modern relation of simultaneity. This carries a presumption of homogeneity that was essentially negated by the dominant time consciousness.[16] I return to this later.

Now the move to what I am calling secularity is obviously related to this radically purged time consciousness. It comes when associations are placed firmly and wholly in homogeneous, profane time, whether or not the higher time is negated altogether or other associations are still admitted to exist in it. Such is the case with the public sphere, and therein lies its new and (close to) unprecedented nature.

I can now perhaps draw this discussion together and try to state what the public sphere *was*. It was a new metatopical space, in which members of society could exchange ideas and come to a common mind. As such, it constituted a metatopical agency, but one that was understood to exist independent of the political constitution of society and completely in profane time.

An extrapolitical, secular, metatopical space: this is what the public sphere was and is. The importance of understanding this lies partly in the fact that it was not the only such space, that it was part of a development that transformed our whole understanding of time and society, so that we have trouble even recalling what it was like before.

T here are, of course, two other such extrapolitical, secular spaces that have played a crucial role in the development of society in the modern West: first, society considered as extrapolitically organized in a (market) economy, which I mentioned above; and second, society as a "people," that is, as a metatopical agency that is thought to preexist and found the politically organized society. We have to see these three as linked in their development, and also as interwoven with other kinds of social spaces that were also emerging at this time.

Habermas notes that the new public sphere brought together people who had already carved out a "private" space as economic agents and owners of property, as well as an "intimate" sphere that was the locus of their family life. The agents constituting this new public sphere were thus both "bourgeois" and "homme."[1]

I think there is a very important link here. The importance of these new kinds of private space, that is, the heightened sense of their significance in human life, and the growing consensus in favor of entrenching their independence in the face of state and church, bestowed in fact exceptional importance on an extrapolitical and secular domain of life. It is hard not to believe that this in some way facilitated the rise of the public sphere.

I would like to place these forms of privacy in a further historical context, which I already invoked above (chapter 5), in connection with the rise of the economy. This is what I have called the "affirmation of ordinary life."[2] By this I mean the broad movement in European culture, which seems to have been carried first by the Protestant Reformation, that steadily enhances the significance of production and family life. Whereas the dominant ethics that descend from the ancient world tended to treat these as infrastructural to the "good life," defined in terms of supposedly higher activities like contemplation or citizen participation, and whereas medieval Catholicism leaned to a view that made the life of dedicated celibacy the highest form of Christian practice, the Reformers stressed that we follow God first of all in our calling and in our family. The ordinary is sanctified, or put in other terms, the claims to special sanctity of certain types of life (the monastic) or special places (churches) or special acts (the Mass) were rejected as part of false and impious belief that humans could in some way control the action of grace.

But to say that all claims to special sanctity were rejected is to say that the nodal points where profane time especially connected with divine time were repudiated. We live our ordinary lives, work in our callings, sustain our families in profane time. In the new perspective, this is what God demands of us, and not an attempt on our part to connect with eternity. That connection is purely God's affair. Thus, the issue of whether we live good or bad lives was henceforth situated firmly in ordinary life and within profane time.

Transposed out of a theological and into a purely human dimension, this gave rise to the constellation of modern beliefs and sensibility that makes the central questions of the good life turn on how we live our ordinary lives, and turns its back on supposedly higher or more heroic modes of life. It underlies the bourgeois ethic of peaceful rational productivity in its polemic against the aristocratic ethic of honor and heroism. It can even appropriate its own forms of heroism, as in the Promethean picture of humans as producers, transforming the face of the earth, which we find with Marx. Or it can issue in the more recent ethic of self-fulfillment in relationships, which is very much part of our contemporary world.

This is the background against which we can understand the two developments Habermas picks out. First, the saliency given to the private economic agent reflects the significance of the life of production in the ethic of ordinary life. This agent is private, as against the public realm of state and other authority. The private world of production now has a new dignity and importance. The enhancing of the private in effect gives the charter to a certain kind of individualism. The agent of production acts on his own, operates in a sphere of exchange with others that doesn't need to be constituted by authority. As these acts of production and exchange come to be seen as forming an ideally self-regulating system, the notion emerges of a new kind of extrapolitical and secular sphere, an economy in the modern sense. Where the word originally applied to the management of a household, and therefore to a domain that could never be seen as self-regulating, in the eighteenth century the notion arises of an economic system, with the physiocrats and Adam Smith, and that is the way we understand it today.

The (market) economy comes to constitute a sphere, that is, a way people are linked together to form an interconnecting society, not only objectively but in their self-understanding. This sphere is extrapolitical and secularly constituted. But it is in an important sense not public. The time has come, perhaps, to distinguish some of the senses of this overworked term.[3]

There seem to be two main semantic axes along which the term public is used. The first connects public to what affects the whole community ("public affairs") or the management of these affairs ("public authority"). The second makes publicity a matter of access ("This park is open to the public") or appearance ("The news has been made public"). The new private sphere of economic agents contrasts with public in the first sense. But these agents also came to constitute a public sphere in the second sense, because this sphere is precisely a metatopical common space, a space in which people come together and contact each other. It is a space, we might say, of mutual appearance, and in that sense a public space.

But the economic sphere proper is not public even in that second sense. The whole set of economic transactions are linked in a series of causal relations, which can be traced and by which we can understand how they influence each other. But this is not a matter of common decision (by public authority), nor do these linked transactions lie in some public domain of common appearance. And yet it is a "sphere" because the agents in an economy are seen as being linked in a single society, in which their actions reciprocally affect each other in some systematic way.

The economy is the first mode of society of the new sort defined above, a society constituted purely extrapolitically and in profane time. It forms part of the background to the rise of the public sphere. It seems very plausible that the explanation of each is interlinked with that of the other.

The second background Habermas picks out is the intimate sphere. Here we see a development of the second main constituent of ordinary life: the world of the family and its affections. As the eighteenth century develops, this becomes the locus of another demand for privacy, this time defined in relation to the second kind of publicness, that concerned with access. Family life retreats more and more into an intimate sphere, shielded from the outside world and even from other members of a large household. Houses are more and more constructed to allow for the privacy of family members in relation to servants as well as outsiders.

The enhanced value placed on family life, in the context of another long-term development toward greater concentration on subjectivity and inwardness, has as one of its fruits the eighteenth-century cherishing of sentiment. Another shift occurs, as it were, in the center of gravity of the good life, within the broad development that affirms ordinary life, and a new importance comes to repose on our experiencing fine, noble, or exalted sentiments. This new ethic both defines and propagates itself through literature. Perhaps its central ve- hicle was the epistolary novel. Rousseau's *Julie* is a paradigm case.

This literature helped define a new understanding of an intimate sphere of close relations: the home at its finest of noble sentiments and exalted experience. This understanding of experience was further enriched by a new conception of art in the category of the aesthetic. This is another fruit of subjectification, of course, because art understood in this category is being defined in terms of our reaction to it. It is in this century that music becomes more and more detached from public and liturgical function and comes to join the other arts as objects of aesthetic enjoyment, enriching the intimate sphere.

This intimate realm was also part of the background against which the public sphere emerged. And not only because it constituted part of the domain of the (extrapolitical and secular) private, but also because the intimate domain had to be defined through public interchange, both of literary works and of criticism. This is only superficially a paradox, as we shall see below. A new definition of human identity, however private, can become generally accepted only through being defined and affirmed in public space. And this critical exchange itself came to constitute a public sphere. We might say it came to constitute an axis of the public sphere, along with, even slightly ahead of, the principal axis of exchange around matters of public (in the first sense) policy. People who never met came to a mutually recognized common mind about the moving power of Rousseau's *Julie*, just as they came to do in the early revolutionary period about the insights of his *Contrat Social*.

There is also a third way in which the Reformation helped to create the conditions for metatopical common agency in secular time. I am thinking here particularly of the more radical, Calvinist wing. From the very beginning, Calvinism usually demanded a much more thoroughgoing reorganization of church life than the more moderate Lutheran variant. Later, particularly in the English-speaking countries, it also spilled over into political restructuring and the founding of new political units designed on new principles, as in New England. At this point, this strand of the Reformation also began to fissure and to generate new "free" churches, based more and more on voluntary associations, a process that intensifies in the eighteenth century with Methodism and the Great Awakening.

In this recurrent activity of founding and refounding, we are witnessing more and more the creation of common agencies in secular time. We still have a crucial reference to God, as the one who calls us to this refounding, but the reference to higher time is less and less prominent. It remained, if at all, only in an eschatological perspective, to the extent that the new reforms were thought to be ushering in the end of profane time and the gathering of all times in God. As this perspective dims, the founding activity is confined more and more exclusively in profane time.

The life of these new churches or sects also helped to set the scene for modern forms of common agency in another respect. They usually demanded a strong commitment from their members, drawing them to associate with others beyond the bounds of family, lineage, neighborhood, and traditional fealty. They created societies in which these more partial ties mattered less than belonging to a religious community for which membership was individual and fundamentally the same for all. Something like this, of course, was always part of the theory of the Christian Church, but the modern sect lived this more intensely and accustomed its members to seeing themselves as belonging individually and directly to the whole. The ground was thus prepared for modern "horizontal" or direct-access societies, in which our membership is unmediated by any partial group, as also for a mode of sociability in which new associations are constantly being created.[4]

It is against this whole economic, ecclesial, and intimate-sentimental background that we have to understand the rise of the public sphere in Europe. This means that we should understand it as part of a family of extrapolitical and secular constitutions of "society." On one side, it relates to the economy, even farther removed from the political realm in that it is not a domain of publicity in any sense. On the other side, it helped to nourish the new images of popular sovereignty, which gave rise to new and sometimes frightening forms of political action in the eighteenth century.

8 The Sovereign People

Popular sovereignty is the third in the great connected chain of mutations in the social imaginary that have helped constitute modern society. It too starts off as a theory, and then gradually infiltrates and transmutes social imaginaries. But how does this come about? We can in fact distinguish two rather different paths. I define them here as ideal types, recognizing that in real historical developments they often are combined and sometimes are difficult to disentangle.

On the one hand, a theory may inspire a new kind of activity with new practices, and in this way form the imaginary of whatever groups adopt these practices. The first Puritan churches formed around the idea of a covenant provide examples of this. A new ecclesial structure flowed from a theological innovation; this becomes part of the story of political change, because the civil structures themselves were influenced in certain American colonies by the ways churches were governed, as with Connecticut Congregationalism, where only the converted enjoyed full citizenship.

Or else the change in the social imaginary comes with a reinterpretation of a practice that already existed in the old dispensation. Older forms of legitimacy are colonized, as it were, with the new understandings of order, and then transformed, in certain cases, without a clear break.

The United States is a case in point. The reigning notions of legitimacy in Britain and America, the ones that fired the English Civil War, for instance, as well as the beginnings of the colonies' rebellion, were basically backward-looking. They turned around the idea of an "ancient constitution," an order based on law holding since time out of mind, in which Parliament had its rightful place beside the king. This was typical of one of the most widespread premodern understandings of order, which referred back to a "time of origins" (Eliade's phrase), which was not in ordinary time.

This older idea emerges from the American Revolution transformed into a full-fledged foundation in popular sovereignty, whereby the U.S. Constitution is put in the mouth of "We, the people." This was preceded by an appeal to the idealized order of natural law, in the invocation of "truths held self-evident" in the Declaration of Independence.[1] The transition was made easier because what was understood as the traditional law gave an important place to elected assemblies and their consent to taxation. All that was needed was to shift the balance in these so as to make elections the only source of legitimate power.

But what has to take place for this change to come off is a transformed social imaginary, in which the idea of foundation is taken out of the mythical early time and seen as something that people can do today. In other words, it becomes something that can be brought about by collective action in contemporary, purely secular time. This happened sometime in the eighteenth century, but really more toward its end than its beginning. Elites had propounded *theories* of founding action beforehand, but these hadn't adequately sunk into the general social imaginary for them to be acted on. So that 1688, radical departure, as it may seem to us in retrospect, was presented as an act of continuity, of return to a preexistent legality. (We are fooled by a change in semantics. The "Glorious Revolution" had the original sense of a return to the original position, not the modern sense of an innovative turnover. Of course, it helped by its *Wirkungsgeschichte* [effect on subsequent history] to alter the sense.)

This fit between new theory and traditional practices was crucial to the outcome. Popular sovereignty could be invoked in the American case because it could find a generally agreed upon institutional meaning. All colonists agreed that the way to found a new constitution was through some kind of assembly, perhaps slightly larger than the normal one, such as in Massachusetts in 1779. The force of the old representative institutions helped to "interpret" in practical terms the new concept.

111

We can say that the American Revolution started on the basis of one legitimacy idea and finished by engendering another, very different one, while somehow avoiding a radical break. The colonists started by asserting the traditional "rights of Englishmen" against an arrogant and insensitive imperial government. Once the break with King in Parliament was consummated and the governors were no longer to be obeyed, the leadership of the resistance passed naturally to the existing elected legislatures, associated in a Continental Congress. The analogy with the Civil War of the 1640s was evident.

But war has always been a source of radicalization. The breach itself was made through a Declaration that affirmed universal human rights, no longer simply those of Englishmen. Certain states adopted new constitutions based on the popular will. Ultimately, the whole movement culminates in a Constitution that places the new republic squarely within the modern moral order: as the will of a people that had no need of some preexisting law to act as a people but could see itself as the source of law.

The new social imaginary comes essentially through a retrospective reinterpretation. The revolutionary forces were mobilized largely on the basis of the old, backward-looking legitimacy idea. This will later be seen as the exercise of a power inherent in a sovereign people. The proof of its existence and legitimacy lies in the new polity it has erected. But popular sovereignty would have been incapable of doing this job if it had entered the scene too soon. The predecessor idea, invoking the traditional rights of a people defined by their ancient constitution, had to do the original heavy lifting, mobilizing the colonists for the struggle, before being relegated to oblivion with the pitiless ingratitude toward the past that defines modern revolutions.

Of course, this didn't mean that nothing changed in the practices, only the legitimating discourse. On the contrary, certain important new steps were taken, which only the new discourse could justify. I've already mentioned the new state constitutions, such as that of Massachusetts in 1779. But the federal Constitution itself is the most striking example. In the Federalist view, it was imperative to create a new central power that wasn't simply a creature of the states; this had been the principal fault of the confederal regime they were trying to replace. There had to be something more than the "peoples" of the different states creating a common instrument. The new union government had to have its own base of legitimacy in a "people of the United States." This was integral to the whole Federalist project.

At the same time, this projection backward of the action of a sovereign people wouldn't have been possible without the continuity in institutions and practices that allowed for the reinterpretation of past actions as the fruit of the new principles. The essence of this continuity resided in the virtually universal acceptance among the colonists of elected assemblies as legitimate forms of power. This was the more heartfelt in that their elected legislatures had long been the main bulwark of their local liberties against the encroachments of an executive under royal or imperial control. At most, come a crucial turning point like the adoption of a new state constitution, they had recourse to special enlarged assemblies. Popular sovereignty could be embraced because it had a clear and uncontested institutional meaning. This was the basis of the new order.[2]

Quite different was the case in the french Revolution, with fateful effects. The impossibility remarked by all historians of "bringing the Revolution to an end"[3] came partly from this, that any particular expression of popular sovereignty could be challenged by some other, with substantial support. Part of the terrifying instability of the first years of the Revolution stemmed from this negative fact, that the shift from the legitimacy of dynastic rule to that of the nation had no agreed meaning in a broadly based social imaginary.

This is not to be understood as the global explanation of this instability, but as telling us something about the way the different factors we cite to explain it worked together to produce the result we know. Of course, the fact that substantial parts of the king's entourage, the army and the nobility, did not accept the new principles created a tremendous obstacle to stabilization. Even those who were for the new legitimacy were divided among themselves. But what made these latter divisions so deadly was the absence of any agreed understanding on the institutional meaning of the sovereignty of the nation.

Burke's advice to the revolutionaries was to stick to their traditional Constitution and amend it piecemeal. But this was already beyond their powers. It was not just that the representative institutions of this Constitution, the Estates General, had been in abeyance for 175 years. They were also profoundly out of synch with the aspiration to equal citizenship that had developed among the educated classes, the bourgeoisie and a good part of the aristocracy, which found expression in a number of ways: negatively through the attack on aristocratic privilege, and positively in the enthusiasm for republican Rome and its ideals.[4] That is why virtually the first demand of the Third Estate in 1789 was to abolish the separate chambers and bring all the delegates together in a single National Assembly.

Even more gravely, outside of these educated elites there was very little sense of what a representative constitution might mean. True, masses of people responded to the calling of the Estates General, with their *cahiers de doléance*, but this whole procedure supposed the continuance of royal sovereignty; it wasn't at all suited to serve as a channel for the popular will.

What the moderates hoped for was something along the lines of Burke's prescription: an evolution of the traditional constitution to fashion the kind of representative institutions that would precisely be understood by all as the expression of the nation's will through the votes of the citizens. This is what the House of Commons had become in the eighteenth century, even though the "people" here was a small elite, deemed to speak for the whole through various modes of virtual representation.

The evolution that had brought this about in Britain had created a sense of the forms of self-rule that was part of the social imaginary of the broader society. That's why the demands for broader popular participation took the form in England of proposals to extend the franchise. The people wanted in to the established representative structure, as is most notable in the Chartist agitation of the 1830s and 1840s. The American case was a stage ahead on this same evolution; their representative assemblies were generally elected on the basis of manhood suffrage.

These forms of self-rule through elected assembly were part of the generally available repertory in the Anglo-Saxon societies. Not only were they absent in that of the popular classes in France, but these had developed their own forms of popular protest that were structured by a quite different logic. But before turning to examine these, there is a general point to be made about modern revolutionary transitions carried out on the basis of novel theories.

The transition can only come off, in anything like the desired sense, if the "people," or at least important minorities of activists, understand and internalize the theory. But for political actors, understanding a theory is being able to put it into practice in their world. They understand it through the practices that put it into effect. These practices have to make sense to them, the kind of sense the theory prescribes. But what makes sense of our practices is our social imaginary. And so what is crucial to this kind of transition is that the people (or its active segments) share a social imaginary that can fill this requirement, that is, that includes ways of realizing the new theory.

We can think of the social imaginary of a people at a given time as a kind of repertory, as I suggested in chapter 2, including the ensemble of practices they can make sense of. To transform society according to a new principle of legitimacy, we have to have a repertory that includes ways of meeting this principle. This requirement can be broken down into two facets: (1) the actors have to know what to do, have to have practices in their repertory that put the new order into effect; and (2) the ensemble of actors have to agree on what these practices are.

To evoke an analogy drawn from Kantian philosophy: theories are like abstract categories; they need to be "schematized," to receive some concrete interpretation in the domain of practice, if they are to be operative in history.

There have been certain modern revolutionary situations where the first facet has been virtually completely missing. Take the Russian case, for instance: the collapse of tsarist rule in 1917 was supposed to open the way to a new republican legitimacy, which the provisional government supposed would be defined in the Constituent Assembly they called for the following year. But if we follow the analysis of Orlando Figes, the mass of the peasant population couldn't conceive of the Russian people as a whole as a sovereign agent.[5] What they did perfectly well understand, and what they sought, was the freedom for the *mir* to act on its own, to divide the land that the nobles (in their view) had usurped, and to no longer suffer repression at the hands of the central government. Their social imaginary included *a local collective agency*, the people of the village or mir. They knew that this agency had to deal with a national government that could do them a lot of harm, and even occasionally some good. But they had no conception of *a national people* that could take over sovereign power from the despotic government. Their repertory didn't include collective actions of this type at this national level; what they could understand was large-scale insurrections, like the Pugachovschina, whose goal was not to take over and replace central power, but to force it to be less malignant and invasive.

By contrast, what was missing in the period of the French Revolution was the second facet. More than one formula was offered to realize popular sovereignty. On one side, the traditional institutions of the Estates General were unsuited for this purpose; the (common) people elected only one chamber out of three; and the whole system was meant to represent subjects making supplication to a sovereign monarch.

But on the other side, the gamut of theories offered was

much wider than in the American case. This was partly due to the fact that in the Anglo-Saxon world, the powerful hold of representative institutions on the imaginary inhibited the theoretical imagination, but it also arose out of the peculiar trajectories of French culture and thought.

Of particular importance in the French case was a range of theories influenced by Rousseau. These had two features that were fateful for the course of the Revolution. The first was what underlay Rousseau's conception of *la volonté générale*. This reflected Rousseau's new and more radical redaction of the modern idea of order.

The principle of this idea of order, as we have seen, is that we are each meant to pursue freely the means to life, but in such a way that each in seeking his own aids—or at least refrains from hindering—the parallel search of others. In other words, our pursuit of our life plans must harmonize. But this harmony was variously conceived. It can come about through invisible hand processes, as with the celebrated theory of Adam Smith.[6] But as this was never thought to suffice, harmonization was also to be brought about consciously, through our following natural law. Locke saw this as given by God, and the motivation for obeying it was whatever makes us obey God: a sense of obligation to our Creator and the fear of eternal punishment.

Later, the fear of God is replaced by the idea of impersonal benevolence, or else by a notion of natural sympathy. But what all these earlier conceptions have in common is that they suppose a duality of motivations in us: we can be tempted to serve our interest at the expense of others, and then we can also be moved—through fear of God, impersonal benevolence or whatever—to act for the general good. It is this dualism that Rousseau wanted to set aside. True harmony can come only when we overcome this duality, when my love of myself coincides with my desire to fulfill the legitimate goals of my co-agents (those participating with me in this harmonization). In Rousseau's language, the primitive instincts of self-love (*amour de soi*) and sympathy (*pitié*) fuse together in the rational and virtuous human being into a love of the common good, which in the political context is known as the general will.

In other words, in the perfectly virtuous man, self-love is no longer distinct from love of others. But the overcoming of this distinction brings with it a new dualism which arises at another point. If self-love is also love of humanity, how to explain the egoistic tendencies that fight in us against virtue? These must come from another motive, which Rousseau calls pride (*amour propre*). So my concern for myself can take two different forms, which are opposed to each other as good is to evil.

This distinction is new in the context of the Enlightenment. But in another sense, it involves a return to a way of thinking deeply anchored in tradition. We distinguish two qualities in the will. We're back in the moral world of Augustine: humans are capable of two loves, one good, the other evil. But it's a revised Augustine, a Pelagian Augustine, if the paradox is not too shocking, because the good will is now innate, natural, entirely anthropocentric, as Monseigneur de Beaumont saw very clearly.

And the theory itself is very modern, placed within the modern moral order. The goal is to harmonize individual wills, even if this can't be done without creating a new identity, a *moi commun*.[7] What has to be rescued is liberty, the individual liberty of each and every one. Freedom is the supreme good, to the point that Rousseau reinterprets the opposition of virtue and vice to align it with that of liberty and slavery: "Car l'impulsion de l'appétit est esclavage, et l'obéissance à une loi qu'on s'est prescrite est liberté."[8] The law we love, because it aims at the good of all, is not a brake on freedom. On the contrary, it comes from what is most authentic in us, from a self-love that is enlarged and transposed into the higher register of morality. It's the fruit of the passage from solitude to society, which is also that from the animal condition to that of humanity:

> Ce passage de l'état de nature à l'état civil produit dans l'homme un changement très remarquable, en substituant dans sa conduite la justice à l'instinct, et donnant à ses actions la moralité qui leur manquait auparavant. . . . Quoiqu'il se prive dans cet état de plusieurs avantages qu'il tient de la nature, il en regagne de si grands, ses facultés s'exercent et se développent, ses idées s'étendent, ses sentiments s'ennoblissent, son âme toute entière s'élève à tel point que si les abus de cette nouvelle condition ne le dégradait souvent au-dessous de celle dont il est sorti, il devrait bénir sans cesse l'instant heureux qui l'en arracha pour jamais, et qui, d'un animal stupide et borné en fit un être intelligent et un homme.[9]

> (The passage from the state of nature to the civil state produces a remarkable change in man by substituting justice for instinct in his conduct and giving his acts the morality they previously lacked. . . . In this state he is deprived of some advantages given to him by nature, but he gains others so great—his faculties are exercised and developed, his ideas are broadened, his feelings are ennobled, his whole soul is uplifted—that if the abuses of this new state did not often degrade him below his previous level, he would constantly have reason to bless the happy moment when he was drawn out of the state of nature forever and changed from a stupid, short-sighted animal into an intelligent being and a man.)

What opposes this law, on the other hand, is not the authentic self, but a will that has been corrupted and turned from its proper course through other-dependence.

The Rousseau redaction gives us a moral psychology very different from the standard conception of the Enlightenment period, which came down from Locke. It not only returns to a will with potentially two qualities, good and evil; it also presents the relation between reason and the good will in a quite different way. The mainstream version sees disengaged reason, which lifts us to a universal standpoint and makes us impartial spectators, as liberating a general benevolence in us, or at least as teaching us to recognize our enlightened self-interest. For Rousseau, however, this objectifying reason is the servant of strategic thinking, and only serves to embroil us more fully in the power calculations that, by trying to control others, in fact make us more and more dependent on them.

This strategic self, which is at one and the same time isolated and eager for others' approval, represses ever further the true self. The struggle for virtue is that attempt to recover a voice that has been buried and almost silenced deep within us. What we need is the exact opposite of disengagement; we need, rather, a reengagement with what is most intimate and essential in ourselves, rendered inaudible by the clamor of the world, for which Rousseau uses the traditional term "conscience."

> Conscience! Conscience! instinct divin, immortelle et céleste voix; guide assuré d'un être ignorant et borné, mais intelligent et libre; juge infaillible du bien et du mal, qui rends l'homme semblable à Dieu, c'est toi qui fais l'excellence de sa nature et la moralité de ses actions; sans toi je ne sens rien en moi qui m'élève au-dessus des bêtes, que le triste privilège de m'égarer d'erreurs en er-

reurs à l'aide d'un entendement sans règle et d'une raison sans principe.[10]

(Conscience! Conscience! Divine instinct, immortal voice from heaven; sure guide for a creature ignorant and finite indeed, yet intelligent and free; infallible judge of good and evil, making man like to God! In thee consists the excellence of man's nature and the morality of his actions; apart from thee, I find nothing in myself to raise me above the beasts—nothing but the sad privilege of wandering from one error to another, by the help of an unbridled understanding and a reason which knows no principle.)

This theory suggested a new kind of politics, which we in fact see enacted in the climactic period of the Revolution, 1792–94. First, it is a politics that makes virtue a central concept, a virtue that consists in the fusion of self-love and love of country. As Robespierre put it in 1792: "L'âme de la République, c'est la vertu, c'est l'amour de la patrie, le dévouement magnanime qui confond tous les intérêts dans l'intérêt général."[11] In one sense, this was a return to an ancient notion of virtue, which Montesquieu had identified as the "mainspring" of republics, "une préférence continuelle de l'intérêt public au sien propre."[12] But it has been reedited in the new Rousseauian terms of fusion ("qui confond tous les intérêts dans l'intérêt général").

Second, it tends to Manichaeanism. The gray areas between virtue and vice tend to disappear. There is no legitimate place alongside for private interest, even if subordinate to the love of the general good. Self-interest is a sign of corruption, thus of vice, and at the limit can become inseparable from opposition. The egoist becomes identified as traitor.

Third, the discourse of this politics has a quasi-religious tenor, as has often been remarked.[13] The sacred is often evoked (*l'union sacrée*, the "sacriligeous hand" that killed Marat, etc.).

But one of the most fateful features of this politics is, fourth, its complex notion of representation. For Rousseau, of course — and this is the second important feature of his theory — political representation expressed in its normal sense through elected assemblies, was anathema. This is connected with his insistence on transparency.[14] The general will is the site of maximum transparency, in the sense that we are maximally present and open to each other when our wills fuse into one. Opacity is inherent to particular wills, which we often try to realize by indirect strategies, using manipulation and false appearances (which touches on another form of representation, of a quasi-theatrical type, which is also bad and harmful). That is why this political outlook so easily assimilates disaffection with hidden and nonavowable action, even with plots, hence at the limit with treason. The general will, on the other hand, is created openly, in the sight of everyone. Which is why, in this type of politics, the general will always has to be defined, declared, one might even say produced before the people, in another kind of theater which Rousseau had clearly described. This is not a theater where actors present themselves before spectators, but rather one modeled on the public festival, where everyone is both performer and spectator. This is what distinguishes the true republican festival from the modern degraded forms of theater. In the former, one may well ask:

> Mais quels seront enfin les objets de ces spectacles? Rien, si l'on veut. Avec la liberté, partout où règne l'affluence, le bien-être y règne aussi. Plantez au milieu d'une place publique un pique couronné de fleurs, rassemblez-y le peuple, et vous aurez une fête. Faites mieux encore: donnez les spectateurs en spectacle; rendez-les acteurs eux-

mêmes; faites que chacun se voie et s'aime dans les autres, afin que tous en soient mieux unis.[15]

(But what will be the objects of these entertainments? What will be shown in them? Nothing, if you please. With liberty, wherever abundance reigns, well-being also reigns. Plant a stake crowned with flowers in the middle of a square; gather the people together there, and you will have a festival. Do better yet; let the spectators become an entertainment to themselves; make them actors themselves; do it so that each sees and loves himself in the others so that all will be better united.)

Transparency, that is nonrepresentation, requires a certain form of discourse, where the common will is defined publicly; and even forms of liturgy where this will is made manifest for and by the people, and that not once and for all but repeatedly, one might even think obsessively. This makes sense of a crucial dimension of revolutionary discourse in these fateful years in Paris, where legitimacy was meant to be won through a (finally right) formulation of that general will that is already, ex ante, that of the healthy and virtuous republic. This goes some way to explain the striking verboseness of the struggle between the factions in 1792–94. But it also shows the importance given to revolutionary festivals, which Mona Ozouf has studied.[16] These were attempts to make the republic manifest to the people, or the people manifest to itself, following Rousseau; these festivals often borrowed their forms from earlier religious ceremonies, such as Corpus Christi processions.

I say that the Rousseauian notion of representation was complex because it involved more than the negative point, the interdict on representative assemblies. We can see in the revolutionary discourse itself, and in the festivals, another kind of representation, discursive or quasi-theatrical. Fair enough, one might say; this doesn't infringe the Rousseauian interdict; the festivals even follow his plan. But there was already something less avowable and more potentially dangerous here. Insofar as the general will exists only where there is real virtue, that is, the real fusion of individual and common wills, what can we say of a situation in which many, perhaps even most people are still "corrupt," that is, have not yet achieved this fusion? Its only locus now will be the minority of the virtuous. They will be the vehicles of the genuine common will, which is objectively that of everyone, that is, the common goals everyone would subscribe to if virtuous.

What is this minority supposed to do with this insight into its own correctness? Just let a corrupt majority "will of all" take its course through the working of certain formally agreed upon procedures of voting? What would be the value of this, for there can as yet by hypothesis be no true republic where the will of all coincides with the general will? Surely the minority is called on to act so as to bring about the true republic, which means to combat corruption and establish virtue.

We can see here the temptation to vanguard politics which has been such a fateful part of our world. This kind of politics involves a claim to representation of a new kind. It's not the old premodern kind, where, in virtue of the structure of things, the king represents his kingdom, the bishop his church, the duke his rear vassals, and so on, because in occupying their place they constitute their subordinates as representable collectivities. It is very different from this, but like these older forms, revolutionary power will use quasi-theatrical forms of self-presentation to make the representative function manifest.

Nor is it representation in the modern sense, which Rousseau condemned, where deputies are chosen by constituents to make decisions binding on all. We might say that this novel, not fully avowed form is rather a kind of representation by "incarnation." The minority embodies the general will and is the only place where this is embodied. But this makes the claim hard to formulate, not only because the minority want to distinguish themselves from the formal model of elected representatives, but also because there is something inherently provisional about this claim to speak for the whole. By hypothesis, it could have no place in a functioning republic. It can play a role only in the revolutionary transition. It is part of the theory of revolution; it has no place in the theory of government.[17] This is the root of that incoherence we always see in the politics of the vanguard, right up to the major twentieth-century example of Bolshevism.

In any case, this only semi-avowed theory of representation by incarnation engendered new political forms. It is what lay behind the new kind of active vanguard clubs, of which the Jacobins are the most celebrated example. Furet, following Augustin Cochin, has shown how important were the *sociétés de pensée* in the run-up to the calling of the Estates General.[18]

We can see here the theoretical basis for a kind of politics that the heady climax of 1792–94 has made familiar to us, and which created a modern tradition we see continued in, for instance, Leninist communism. It is a politics of virtue, as the fusion of individual and general will, and it is Manichaean, highly "ideological," even quasi-religious in tone. It seeks transparency and hence fears its polar opposite, hidden agendas and plots. And it practices two forms of representation: first, in both discursive and quasi-theatrical forms, it makes manifest the general will; second, even if only implicitly, it lays claim to a kind of representation by incarnation.

Obviously, this politics couldn't follow the integral Rousseauian prescriptions. It couldn't, for instance, go along with his absolute ban on representative assemblies. That was evidently unworkable in a large sprawling country of almost 30 million. But the Rousseauian suspicion of assemblies was still at work in Jacobin practice, in particular when they mobilized the people of Paris in the sections to act against, and even to purge, the Assembly, as in May–June 1793. Here, direct action by the people was meant to trump a (partially) corrupt representative institution.

The potentially explosive consequences of this theory and the practices it inspired can be understood if we place it back in the context defined earlier. This is the context defined by the negative facts: first, there was, unlike in the United States, no preexisting consensus in the social imaginary about what rule by the people meant in institutional terms; and second, the stability that even an illogical, heteroclite compromise with royal power might have provided, because of its continuity with the past, was fatally jeopardized by the underhand opposition of Louis and his entourage. In this framework, the gamut of theories about popular sovereignty becomes very important; in particular, the fact that this gamut includes the radical Rousseau-derived version had fateful consequences.

Does this mean that we are blaming the "excesses" of 1792–94, in particular the Terror, on the ideology espoused by revolutionaries? That would be rather too simple. There is one more important facet of the whole transition that we have to take account of. We have not only new political forms and practices, spawned by theory; there are also older practices that were taken up under a new interpretation. These were the modes of popular protest and revolt that had developed among nonelites in ancien régime France. These were structured by their own logic.

French peasants and city dwellers had their own way of making their needs known when things got intolerable: the peasant or urban uprising. In towns, when, say, the price of wheat soared and local merchants were suspected of hoarding grain to make a killing, riots could break out, targeting the municipal authorities and/or the offending merchants. These offenders were often killed, in a partly ritualized violence which our modern sensibility finds gruesome (e.g., the victims decapitated, their heads carried around on pikes and displayed). Then the royal government would react, send in some soldiers, restore order, and make some exemplary punishments (more killing, with its own ritual elements, which accompanied public executions under the ancien régime).[19] But they would also be sure to take measures to lower the price of grain, imposing ceilings and importing stocks from elsewhere.

From one point of view, one can see the whole bloody process as an exchange between the base and the summit where power resides, the enacting of a cahier de doléance in unmistakable terms. But the background understanding that enframes the whole exchange is that power remains at the summit—the very opposite of the understanding defining popular sovereignty. The revolt as such laid no claim to popular power.[20] On the contrary, the people often fed on the age-old myth that the good king had been betrayed by his local agents and officers, and that one needed to redress the situation in his name. Thus, in 1775, rioters seized stocks and forcibly fixed prices, supposedly "par l'ordre du roi."[21] Popular classes that function in this way have to transform their repertory before they can act as a sovereign people.

A good part of what was involved in "bringing the Revolution to an end" was this transformation of the popular repertory, the development of a new social imaginary that would confer on regular ordered elections the meaning of expressions of popular will. In the meantime, as always, there was a struggle to reinterpret old practices in a new way.

Take the storming of the Bastille on 14 July 1789. This was in many ways an old-style popular insurrection. It had a particular, limited goal: getting hold of the arms supposedly stored in the Bastille in order to defend Paris against the threat of the Swiss mercenaries. And it ended in a traditional ritual of violence: the execution of the governor, whose head was displayed on a pike. But just as the revolt of the colonies in the name of their traditional, established rights was later reinterpreted as the innovative act of a sovereign people, so here the taking of the Bastille was seen as an assertion of popular power. The building's importance was no longer the particular, contingent fact that it contained arms (actually, it didn't, but that was what was believed), but its essential, symbolic nature as a prison in which people were arbitrarily confined by royal fiat.

In fact, as William Sewell has shown, the action provoked at first a certain malaise in the Assembly and among the elites.[22] Everyone was happy with the result (the retreat of the royal troops) but rather reticent, if not downright disapproving of the methods used. This was the kind of outbreak of popular violence that the propertied classes always feared and that the reform of the Constitution was meant to avoid. It was only later that the action was given a new interpretation, as an expression of the popular will and of the people's sovereign right to defend itself. This was the basis of a new practice, that of the revolutionary insurrection. It was destined to have a long and often bloody career, as we now know. But the new form, and the imaginary that animates it, could not have taken hold that quickly without the continuity linking it to the long tradition of urban uprisings.[23]

This creative misremembering has played a big part in the transformation of the social imaginary. It was ritually referred to in the Fête de la Fédération exactly a year later, through which Lafayette hoped to stabilize the revolution in the more moderate form of a constitutional monarchy. And it has, of course, become *the* symbolic date of the turnover to popular rule, the annual national feast of the French Republic.

Thus, in both cases of retrospective reinterpretation, the American and the French, the new imaginary owes a debt to a more archaic one, which has assumed part of the burden of bringing to existence the new forms, be it the federal constitution or the revolutionary tradition. In return, the new imaginary bears the marks of its origin: the primacy of representative forms in the American case, and a glorification of popular insurrection in the French context, even in a sense a liturgy of revolt. In the long run, the challenge was somehow to unify this tradition of noble insurrection with a commitment to stable representative institutions.

In the nature of things, this kind of transformation couldn't be effected right away, in the immediate aftermath of the Revolution. The original, untransformed culture of popular insurrection continued to weigh heavily on the course of events. It is worthwhile, therefore, to examine a bit more closely the culture of popular revolts. This is a very wide subject. There is the whole issue of rural rebellions, which had their own very powerful impact on the course of the Revolution, but it was the urban uprisings that impinged directly on the battle between the factions in the capital.

If we look at food riots, for example, it is clear that they were based on a popular conception of the normal price. This was a key element of what has been called "the moral economy" of the popular strata, that is, the normative, often implicit, conception of economic relations that the people shared and that underlay their hostility to developing capitalism.[24] Of course, no one expected these norms to be integrally realized. The people were too conscious of the weight of oppressive institutions and powers: nobles, rich merchants, tax farmers, and so on. But when the situation became really intolerable, they felt they had to intervene.

The fact that a price was "abnormal" could always be explained by a culpable and identifiable human agency. Often, the culprit was the "engrosser" (*accapareur*), the merchant who held back stocks in order to raise prices and make a killing; but sometimes the targets of popular wrath were government agents, in cahoots with merchants, or as prime culprits by virtue of having neglected their duty to bring adequate stocks of food in time. In the popular mentality, though, incompetence or lack of vigilance was less the problem than ill will. Public officers who failed in their duty were seen less as inept than as enemies of the common people. This explains how easy it was during the Revolution to explain shortages in terms of an aristocratic plot. Not foul-up but ill will is responsible for misfortunes.

Two things seem crucial to this mentality. First, it leaves very little place for impersonal mechanisms. It had no place for the new conception of the economy, where shortage and glut are explained by a certain state of the market, which in turn can be affected by events in distant lands. If prices rise, it's because the engrosser is hiding stocks to exact a higher tribute from us. Of course, people knew that harvests could be good or bad, and that in this sense, shortages were also natural phenomena. But they thought that within certain limits, the powers in charge were able to bring the necessary supplies from elsewhere to avoid at least the most dramatic hikes. This was another sign, if one likes, that theirs was a mentality of subjects, who tend to attribute to their rulers powers that they don't in fact have. This is also clearly a mentality at the antipodes of capitalism, because it has no place for an economy ordered by impersonal laws, central to the new political economy; besides, it tends to demand an interventionist remedy for every evil.

This belief in the power of direct intervention reflects the second important facet of this mind-set: if things go wrong, it's always someone's fault. One can identify the evildoer and act against him. What's more, because the responsible agent is always an evildoer—not the unconscious and unwilling cause of some misfortune, but a malevolent, even criminal agent—action against him means not just neutralizing his action, but also punishing him. An elementary sense of justice demands this. But there was something more: retribution often has the sense not only of punishing a wrong, but of purging a noxious element.

It's this last factor that perhaps explains why punishments were often extreme and violent; an engrosser could be put to death, for instance. But it also makes sense of the symbolic, quasi-ritual dimension of punishments, including capital punishment—as though the goal was to eliminate the evil at a symbolicomagical level, at the same time as one neutralized it in the form of a concrete adversary one put out of action. We are in the (to us strange) world of ancien régime penal law, with its different forms of "honorable amends," which aimed in some way to undo the crime at a symbolic level. One gets a vivid sense of this if one reads Foucault's riveting and disturbing account of the punishment of Damiens, who was guilty of attempted regicide against Louis XV.[25]

In short, one could say that in this mind-set, the guilty party was often also a scapegoat. Soboul tells the following example:

> Meurtre du bouc-émissaire: ceux de Berthier de Sauvigny, intendant de Paris, et de son beau-père Foullon de Doué, conseiller d'État, le 22 juillet 1789, place de Grève. Ce dernier aurait un jour déclaré que si le peuple manquait de pain, il n'avait qu'à manger du foin. Arrêté à Vitry, il fut amené à l'Hôtel-de-Ville de Paris "ayant un bouquet d'orties sous le menton, raconte Hardy, de l'herbe dans la bouche et devant lui comme cabriolet une botte de foin." Lafayette ayant, du balcon de l'Hotel-de-Ville, proposé "à tous ceux qui consentiraient que le

sieur Foullon fût conduit en prison de lever la main,"
la foule se récria: "Pendu, Pendu, point de prison!"
Foullon est saisi, trîné place de Grève "où il est aussitôt
pendu à la corde d'un réverbère et élevé à la hauteur de
trente pieds, mais cette corde ayant cassé et après l'avoir
raccrochée à plusieurs reprises, on lui coupa enfin la tête
que l'on mit au bout d'une pique." Berthier dut baiser
la tête de son beau-père, puis il fut massacré. Comble
de l'humiliation: les cadavres furent traînés nus dans
les rues.[26]

(Murder of the scapegoat: of Berthier de Sauvigny, Intendant of Paris, and of his father-in-law Foullon de
Doué, state counsellor, on the 22 July 1789 at the place
de Grève. The latter was reported as saying that if the
people lacked bread, they had only to eat hay. Arrested
at Vitry, he was brought to the Hôtel-de-Ville of Paris
"with a bouquet of nettles under his chin," as Hardy tells
it, "grass in his mouth, and in front of him as a carriage a
bundle of hay." Lafayette having proposed, from the bal-
cony of the Hôtel de Ville, "to all those who agreed that
le Sieur Foullon should be taken to prison to raise their
hands," the mob cried out: "hang him, hang him, no
prison!" Foullon is seized, dragged to the place de Grève
"where he was hanged by a rope from a lamp-post and
lifted to the height of thirty feet, but the rope broke and
after stringing him up several times they cut his head off
and put it on a pike." Berthier had to kiss the head of
his father-in-law, and then he was massacred. Utter humiliation: the corpses were dragged naked through the
streets.)

We can see in this mise-en-scène a cruel and gruesome
sense of humor. Foullon is forced himself to play the part of
eater of hay, the lot he supposedly wished on the people. But

the fact that the ceremony of honorable amends takes place in an atmosphere of celebration, something to be enjoyed, and as an affirmation of popular power, doesn't in any way contradict its symbolic power of purification. We know many other contexts where premodern ceremonies have this double aspect, where popular festiveness in no way contradicts ritual efficacy. Carnivals stand as paradigm examples. In fact, even speaking of a double aspect reflects our disenchanted modern "serious" mentality, where the religious and the spiritual suit ill with laughter and spontaneity. Our outlook reflects the long repression of the religion of our ancestors which has made us "modern." Soboul himself, speaking of a less extreme punishment often meted out to engrossers, the sack of their house or shop, says: "L'incendie accompagne souvent le saccage, mais il revêt une signification autrement symbolique: son pouvoir de destruction à la fois spectaculaire et total lui confère une valeur quasi-magique, certainement purificatrice. C'est par le feu que le peuple en révolte détruit tous les symboles d'oppression et de misère: les postes de guet en août 1788; les barrières de l'octroi parisien, dès avant la prise de la Bastille; les terriers lors de la Grande Peur, et quelques châteaux par la même occasion."[27] (Fire often accompanies the sack, but it has a more powerful symbolic meaning: its power of destruction at once spectacular and total gives it an almost magic force, certainly a purifying one. It is by fire that the people in revolt destroy all the symbols of oppression and misery: the watch posts in August 1788; the customs barriers in Paris even before the taking of the Bastille; the feudal records at the time of the Great Fear, and some chateaux on the same occasion.)

The fact that Foullon's words, simple words, seemed to merit such an extreme sentence certainly has something to do with the revolutionary context. But it also reflects the accent put on the ill will of the evildoer in the popular outlook. What he did was not all that serious, even though he was related to the intendant, a royal officer and thus suspect. But his (supposed) words were the purest possible expression of hostility and contempt.

What light does this culture of popular insurrection shed on the course of the Revolution, and particularly on the *dérapage* of 1792–94, the slide into Terror? Once one abandons the attempt to explain the Terror simply by the external circumstances of war and regional armed resistance—and Furet has shown convincingly that these accounts aren't really convincing[28]—one may be tempted to explain it in ideological terms, in relation to the theories that animated the more radical groups, principally the Jacobins and Robespierre. These were not without effect, but a straight ideological account is much too simple.

What this leaves out of account is the immense weight of the popular elements in Paris, often called the *sans-culottes*, on the course of events. They had, in fact, great leverage, because their support was essential at various points to the Revolution, even to its survival, and because, until Thermidor, they could decisively intervene in the battle between factions.

We can formulate the first of these relations in different ways. We could say that the sans-culottes "saved" the Revolution, because at certain crucial moments when counterrevolutionary forces threatened to crush it, popular action tipped the balance. This is certainly a plausible reading of the situation of July 1789, when the king was sending troops toward Paris and the popular uprising induced him to retreat.

Or we can see the relation of forces from another angle. As it was out of the question for the revolutionary elites to appeal to the royalist armed forces, either inside or outside of the country, they could find themselves faced by popular movements they couldn't suppress. This is what happened on 10 August 1792, and recurrently in more or less menacing forms until Thermidor. Indeed, the specter of an uncontrollable popular uprising was laid to rest only at the 18th Brumaire. The situation was particularly dramatic during the September massacres of 1792. The bourgeois leaders of the republic were far from approving; more, they were filled with horror. But they felt powerless, short of an appeal to royalist armed forces, which was inconceivable and very likely would have been suicidal for them.

So they were forced, not only to let things happen, but even to take the lead of the popular movement, to put into practice their own version, better controlled, more moderate (they hoped), of the popular program. This included some element of terror; hence there had to be Terror. As Danton put it the following year: "Profitons des fautes de nos prédécesseurs; faisons ce que n'a pas fait l'Assemblée Législative: soyons terribles pour dispenser le peuple de l'être"[29] (Let's profit from the mistakes of our predecessors; let's do what the Legislative Assembly failed to do: let us practice terror in order to dispense the people from practicing it). But the motive was not really indulgence for the delicate feelings of the people; it was basically a question of survival.

Then, by the dynamic of rivalries, survival comes to be defined more and more narrowly. At the beginning, it is the existence of the Revolution that is at stake; later, what is crucial is the survival of a party self-identified with the Revolution, then of factions of the party, right up to the ultimate collapse in a less menacing military context on 9 Thermidor. As the revolutionaries turn on each other, the people become arbiters, which is the second mode of dependency described above.

All this meant that, for a time, the aspirations and outlook of the popular milieux of Paris had an important influence on the measures and forms of government of the Revolution. The social elites never lost control. There was no repeat of Münster 1536. We could even say that the miracle of this whole period of radical politics was that the Convention, even though purged and intimidated, nevertheless remains theoretically in control of the situation, which is what allowed it to put an end to this whole period at Thermidor. One might say that, paradoxically, it is perhaps the genius of Robespierre as a political maneuverer that explains this survival of parliamentary forms.

But for a while, the revolutionary elites had to go along with popular aspirations and goals, much farther than they would have liked. Even the Robespierriste minority, when forced to adopt certain anticapitalist measures of economic control, clearly were acting with great reluctance.

This means that the period of revolutionary extremism has a double source. One source is certainly in the discourse and theory of the model drawn from Rousseau; but it also has its roots in the mentality of popular revolt. And there were many points where the two outlooks ran parallel.

The suspicion of representation was one such point. It was easy to convince the sans-culottes that popular sovereignty finds a paradigm expression in direct action, although even then, the past weighed heavily. In the crucial *journées* of popular revolt, the leadership and program had to be supplied by the elites. In the one great exception, the post-Thermidor journée of March 1795, the people, once they had surrounded the Convention, became strangely passive, as though they didn't know without guidance what to do next.[30] The old model was still working, where insurrection was meant to induce power to take the necessary action rather than to take control.

Moreover, the moralism, the Manichaeanism of the Rousseauian ideology touched a popular chord. That mere disaffection could be turned into treason fit well with the belief that every misfortune had some malevolent cause. And the tendency to see a plot behind every misfortune was common to both popular culture and elite ideology. Indeed, it may be that the convergence here was itself the result of mutual influence. The popular rhetoric of plots and conspiracies started early, put into circulation by demagogues like Marat. This may have helped to form the revolutionary ideology itself.

But the most striking convergence lies in the Terror itself. This was a violence directed against the agents of misfortune, seen as enemies, as traitors worthy of punishment. But as time went on, Robespierre gave a greater and greater place to the discourse of virtue and of purification. The last great bout of the Terror, in the weeks before Thermidor, was justified by the need to purge the republic of vice, so that it could emerge in all its purity.

Put in other terms, both popular culture and elite ideology converged on a doctrine of the scapegoat. The Terror was a kind of synthesis of these two, a compromise formation, if this psychoanalytic term can be allowed. To this synthesis each side brought something. We might argue that the extreme potentiality of a Rousseauian politics of virtue to turn to violence and purgation, which might never have emerged in a context where the elites remained in control, was brought to realization by the need to lead through following the popular strata.

At the same time, the popular impulse to punishment and purgation was itself purged of its magicosymbolic elements. It was "modernized" and "rationalized." That means that it was given, first, a rational, moral basis: only those who really deserved to die were targeted according to the rational theory of virtue and purification. Second, the punishment itself was carried out in a rational, "clean" form, through a modern, "scientific" instrument, the guillotine, replacing the gory symbolism of the ancien régime. Third, the ritual was purged of all that mixture of the festive and the murderous, the carnival promiscuity of laughter and killing, which was integral to traditional popular culture. One applies rational criteria; one applies them in cold blood after due deliberation; and one deals death in a direct, almost clinical fashion, by means of a modern, efficient machine.

It's as though the institution of scapegoating had gone through its own disenchanting Reformation, made fit for the Age of Reason. Small wonder that Robespierre's discourse of reason comes to resemble more and more an unprecedented form of madness. This seems to be where the Incorruptible had arrived by the summer of 1794. Prisoner of his **138** own discourse, really obsessed by a myth that at the outset was perhaps only a necessary rationalization, he flees forward toward more and more extravagant projects, where the hope of defining once and for all the metaphysical basis of things, with the feast of the Supreme Being, runs alongside tumbrels loaded with more and more victims.[31]

This couldn't last, and came to an end with Thermidor. But it has left us with a troubling legacy: the link between democratic revolution and scapegoating violence. This link reappears in new contexts in the intervening two centuries. It always self-destructs but never seems to disappear for good. It is one of the most disquieting features of modernity.[32]

Thus, the two great eighteenth-century revolutions inaugurated the age of popular sovereignty in terms of the interplay of social imaginaries, new and traditional, which helped determine their respective courses. This interplay was particularly complex, conflictual, and fraught with unforeseen compromises between the old and the new.

Moreover, the French Revolution failed to produce a solution to the problem it set itself: how to produce a stable institutional expression for the new legitimacy idea it espoused, popular sovereignty. This in turn would require the development of a widely shared social imaginary making sense of these institutions.

The great battle between the different revolutionary factions turned on this issue: What was the correct institutional expression for the sovereignty of the nation? This question defined the terms of the struggle between them. Each had its formula to offer as the proper way of realizing this principle: whether through a republic or a constitutional monarchy, through indirect representation or some more immediate relation of people and deputy, through the representation of different interests or the undivided expression of a general will. The undecidable issue between these different institutions and procedures had in the end to be determined at the boundary of all of them, through coups de force. Thus, the members of the Convention elected by the people were eventually purged in 1793 under threat of the activists from the Paris sections, and that in the name of the people.

The terms of this struggle — its peculiarly intense ideological nature, the immense importance placed on theoretical justification and models of right government, during those days when the urgent practical dangers of foreign invasion and internal counterrevolutionary insurrection seemed to demand their place at the top of the agenda — are to be understood in this context. The discourse wasn't simply a cover for the hard reality of group interest and military defense, a diagnosis that becomes truer later, under the Directory. Rather, all this talk was for real, its goal being to establish that one's own group was carrying out the only legitimate realization of the sovereignty of the people. This meant that however dotty the content of the discourse, it was generally meant in deadly earnest, even when we're dealing with the Jacobins, where the criteria of genuine representation of the people turned crucially on the virtue of the leaders, standing foursquare for the whole against the self-interested, divisive factions. It is especially in the case of the Jacobins that the expression "deadly earnest" becomes appropriate.

As Furet has argued, the murderous craziness of the revolutionary crisis cannot be considered a kind of rhetorical froth thrown up by the real battles for national survival, or between groups. We have to allow for its centrality,[33] even while recognizing that this rhetorical battle was bent into strange and frightening shapes by the immense force field set up by popular culture, its demands and expectations.

The problem of "ending the Revolution" continued to haunt French society into the Restoration and well into the nineteenth century.[34] The return to some stability in the aftermath of the Revolution could come only through some generally accepted forms of representative government. This meant solving the double problem that the whole revolutionary period had left unresolved: coming to an agreement among political elites on representative institutions, which could at the same time become part of the popular social imaginary.

Once again, during the Restoration, the opposition of the royalist ultras made things exceedingly difficult. And the growing social divisions that came with the growth of the working class made it all the more difficult to bridge the gap between elite constitutionalism and popular repertory. On the contrary, the Revolution remained alive for a number of radicals not just as the gateway to a proper institutional order, but as itself the paradigm moment of popular sovereignty. Something like a revolutionary scenario, what Robert Tombs calls "the Revolutionary passion play," haunted the radical imagination and remained in the popular memory, waiting to be reenacted in order finally to realize the promise of 1789.[35] In these circumstances, the specter of renewed revolution could never be finally laid to rest, however often the claim was made to have "ended the Revolution."

But as Guizot, the Doctrinaires, Thiers, and later Gambetta saw, the only solution would be the evolution of forms that would come to be generally recognized as the obviously appropriate realization of the new principle of legitimacy. Guizot and the Doctrinaires understood that this required the growth of a new, widely shared social imaginary, but their own elite representative institutions, with their narrow franchise, could never crystallize this around themselves, as gradually became clear after 1830.[36]

Over time, republican France found such forms, but only after it had gone over to manhood suffrage. Gambetta saw that the only way the people could develop a new social imaginary around ordered representative institutions was by participating in their election.[37]

But the forms that took hold in France turned out to be interestingly different from the Anglo-American mode. Pierre Rosanvallon has traced the peculiar path by which universal suffrage was achieved in France, and he brings to light the different shape of the social imaginary in this republican tradition.[38]

This third of the great mutations, after the economy and the public sphere, involves "inventing the people" as a new collective agency.[1] We can recognize in the forms that have emerged from these mutations the lineaments of our understanding of moral order in contemporary liberal democracies. The way we imagine our social life is articulated in these forms. The society in which we live is not just the politically structured order; we also belong to civil society. We are linked in an economy, can seek access to a public sphere, and move in a world of independent associations.

These forms were firmly established in the social imaginary of the leading Western societies before the end of the eighteenth century. But a great distance still separates us today from even the most advanced of those societies; the long march still had a great distance to travel.

One way to indicate the distance is to note that these modes of social imaginary were still the property of minorities: social elites and activist groups. The majority of the populations, certainly in England and France but to some extent also in the United States, were still at least partly immersed in older forms. The stretch of the long march still to come involved a spreading, downward and outward, of these new forms of self-understanding.

But the distance can also be described in other terms. We could say that the modern moral order had reshaped the social imaginary in some dimensions of social life — politics, economy, public sphere — but that other dimensions remained untransformed. The family is one obvious example, but that can't be taken simply on its own. What we now think of as the family was then often embedded in what we could call the household, in which nonkin, or at least nonmembers of the core group, lived and also worked together with the nuclear family: servants, apprentices, a nephew sent to be taught a trade, some employees. These households were often highly patriarchal, under the uncontested authority of the male head, and ruled by a strong sense of hierarchy. Nor did dependency relations stop there; tenants lived in a sort of dependence on landlords and artisans on patrons; even household heads could stand in a relation of dependence on powerful sponsors higher up in the hierarchy who had secured for them their pension or their office or their living, in the case of clergymen. Indeed, these sponsors might depend in turn on even more powerful figures at court or among grandees or in the governor's mansion.

In short, the premodern North Atlantic societies were traversed by chains of dependence of vassalage, patronage, servitude, or (in the family) patriarchy. These chains linked to each other, so that one could trace a line of dependence running from the meanest churl, through the head of his household, to the landholder for whom the latter farmed, up through the patron on which this squire depended for certain favors, ending at the summit in the king. Presented in the most defensible way, all these chains were meant to exhibit a principle of hierarchical complementarity; people at different levels made their own essential contribution to each other's well-being, inferiors providing service, while superiors provided rule and protection.

Seen in this light, there was a continuity, a homogeneity between the structure of the monarchic polity and the various skeins of dependence that were woven together in the society, household, families, clientage, and so on. That is why it was possible to offer paternal power as a standard trope for all forms of dependence based on hierarchical complementarity. According to one of the most widely accepted justifications, royal power was itself to be seen as a species of paternal power; it was similarly natural and independent of subjects' consent. This was the basis of the theory of Robert Filmer, one of the most influential articulators of royal absolute power in the English seventeenth century, whose main work, *Patriarchy*, was pilloried by Locke in his *First Treatise of Civil Government*. But the patriarchal metaphor for royal power was extremely widespread up to the eighteenth century: "The Obedience of Parents is the Basis of all Government," as Addison put it in *The Spectator*.[2] Indeed, the debate prior to the Declaration of Independence in the colonies saw both sides using the image. For Tories, those pondering rebellion were potential parricides, but for many of the future rebels, their action was justified because the Crown had betrayed its parental obligation through its "long chain of abuses."

This society of pervasive paternal power was not just different from our own in being hierarchical; it also related very differently to its members. The crucial point about long chains of dependence is that they were highly personalized. I, a churl, am not just a subject of the king like all others; I am the servant of a particular master, who relates to a particular lord, who relates to a patron, and so on. My subordination to the king is mediated through these particular, personal relations. The power of the patriarchal trope comes partly from this pervasive personalization of power and dependence. Equality, as Tocqueville saw, has gone along with a shattering of these chains and an atomization in which citizens relate to power in an unmediated fashion.[3]

This premodern dispensation was unlike what was emerging in the late eighteenth century, resembling more what we know today, in that the social imaginary was animated through all its dimensions and levels by a similar principle, that of hierarchical complementarity, just as today's is thoroughly penetrated at all levels and niches by the modern moral order. Moreover, this uniformity was not just a fact we can observe; it was itself part of the social imaginary, that is, the agents themselves were aware of the analogies, and that is why they could appeal to paternal power as a trope for kingly authority. Similarly today, we feel the need to criticize and even transform many of our nonpolitical relations, those that are insufficiently "democratic" or egalitarian. We find ourselves speaking of the democratic as against authoritarian family, for instance. We see ourselves as equally consistent as our premodern forebears were, only our lives are organized around a contrary principle.

But the emerging forms of the modern social imaginary that I have been describing seem to us odd, even suspect, because they were introducing a new principle at certain crucial levels — polity, public sphere, economy — while leaving other niches untouched. The people of the time can easily seem to us to be inconsistent, even hypocritical. Elite males spoke of rights, equality, and the republic, but thought nothing of keeping indentured servants, not to speak of slaves, and kept their women, children, their households in general under traditional patriarchal power. Didn't they see the glaring contradiction?

The answer is that this was not necessarily a contradiction. Once one has accepted the background structuring idea that the social imaginary ought to be animated by a uniform principle in all niches, then the differences in the ordering of, say, polity and family stand out. But it is quite possible for people to find this background idea extravagant and implausible, even to fail to consider it as a possibility. In the epoch we are considering, for instance, patriarchy was so deeply rooted in families/households that the republican challenge to monarchical rule and aristocratic hierarchy had to take the form of a denial of the uniform application of the paternal principle, rather than the offering of an opposing principle valid for all niches. Locke's famous answer to Filmer was to distinguish patriarchal from political power and to demonstrate that they operated on quite different principles.[4] And this was the line generally adopted by revolutionaries and reformers. A few brave and innovative figures, like Mary Wollstonecraft, stand out from the virtually unanimous consensus on this. Indeed, it took us a long time to come to see the family, specifically the husband-wife relation in the now nuclear family, outside of the older household framework, in a critical democratic-egalitarian light. This happened, as it were, only yesterday. Uniformity across niches is far from an obvious, common-sense requirement.[5]

Nevertheless, we have come to that uniformity; the long march has finally taken us there. But it came not so much because of a natural drive to consistency. It was more the drive to inclusion, on the part of certain strata that initially were marginalized in the new order. This is the last phase of the long march: on the one hand, the extension of the new social imaginary below and beyond the social elites who originally adopted it; and on the other, the extension of the principles of this new imaginary to other levels and niches of social life. We can see right away that the first is impossible without the second; servants and subordinates can't be inducted into an imaginary that gives them a place among those equal individuals who make up society unless the social forms of subordination tying them to their betters are transformed. There has to be a break with these old forms, in which equality replaces hierarchy, and in which at the same time the personalized, particular relations of the old dependencies are dissolved and replaced by a general and impersonal recognition of equal status.

This transformation came about in most North Atlantic societies, but it happened by different routes and with significantly different inflections. The first and most spectacular case was the United States. This was, in a sense, a revolution within the Revolution, or perhaps better, in the aftermath of the Revolution.[6] One can perhaps describe it as a process by which independence evolves from being a value to be realized by a republican society in relation to external monarchical authority, to being a status to be sought by individuals and enjoyed by all of them equally.

The Revolution had been led by gentlemen, many of them of recent promotion to this rank,[7] but nevertheless gentlemen. They operated in a world in which it was natural that leaders and elected representatives be from the better sort; indeed, the prestige of the offices in question (representative, judge, etc.) was bound up with the social eminence of their holders. Moreover, this revolutionary leadership shared the republican outlook current in the eighteenth century that these leaders should embody "virtue" in the Montesquieuian sense, be dedicated to the public good, and be "disinterested," and that in a way ordinary people, occupied with getting the means to life, couldn't manage. Even engaging in trade made one suspect on this score.[8]

That the United States would go on being governed by such a republican elite was the dream of many in the generation that made the Revolution and designed the Constitution; this dream, of course, supposed the continuance of various forms of nonpolitical subordination, master-servant relations, submissive sons, and deference. But it was not to be. The new revolution was partly a political affair. The political class was invaded by people of all social origins, some conspicuously lacking in gentility, as Jeffersonian Republicans successfully challenged the Federalist elites. But the new personal independence was partly a social transformation, going along with rapid economic growth, the expansion of the internal market, the growth of manufactures, and above all, the opening of the frontier. Independence became a reality for large numbers of young men and often also women, who could and did strike out on their own, leaving their families, and often breaking with their communities and with the traditional ties of dependence.

A certain penchant for materialist explanations may tempt us to explain the new culture of personal independence and equality by these economic and demographic changes. But the inadequacy of such accounts is glaringly evident from the fact that, for instance, the opening of the frontier had rather different cultural consequences just a few miles north, in Canada.[9]

Another common error, the attraction of a subtraction account, may tempt us to define the change merely negatively, as consisting in the dissolution of old ties, submissions, and solidarities. But this independence was not just the breaking of old moral ties; it carried its own moral ideals, as Tocqueville noted in relation to individualism in the modern world.[10] Moreover, the new ideal involved a new kind of link to society. The new character ideal, as Appleby describes it, exalts "the man who developed inner resources, acted independently, lived virtuously, and bent his behaviour to his personal goals."[11] He was a person capable of industry, perseverance, and self-reliance.

The nature of this moral ideal can be gauged partly by its frequent combination with a new piety. The early nineteenth century was the age of the second Great Awakening, the spreading of revival through itinerant preachers all over the republic, to the most remote frontier. The new religious fervor, most often outside the old establishments, in the rapidly growing denominations of Methodists and Baptists, was itself a reflection of the ideal of independence. Individuals broke away from ancestral churches and sought their own forms among the rapidly multiplying denominational options.[12] At the same time, they sought the strength to live this new independence, to beat back the demons of fear and despair, the temptations of idleness and drink (this last was especially potent at a time when Americans drank per capita four times what they do today)[13] in a personal relation of devotion to God. This is a pattern that has become familiar today, in the rapid spread of evangelical Protestantism in many parts of the globe: Latin America, Africa, Asia, the ex-communist countries, not to speak of continuing revivals in the United States.[14] This is not to say that the new personal independence was intrinsically bound up with religious faith. On the contrary, it took all sorts of forms, including very secularized ones, although revivalism was extremely widespread, touching one quarter of the population in this period.[15] But the fact that it could exist in symbiosis with this ardent faith testifies to the moral nature of the ideal.

But personal independence was not just a moral ideal for individual lives; it also related the agent to society. This reference back to society partly consisted in the fact that self-disciplined, honest, imaginative, entrepreneurial people were seen as the cornerstone of the new society, which combined order and progress. They were its chief benefactors, at once setting its moral tone and conferring the immense benefits of economic progress. This assumed, of course, that commerce and entrepreneurship were not divisive, but rather redounded to the good of all and could be the basis of unity for a people who were energetic, disciplined, and self-reliant. It was this kind of drive to progress that was making America great, free, and equal. Personal independence becomes part of a new model of American patriotism, which has remained alive and powerful today.

This represented a tremendous cultural revolution away from the ideals of the revolutionary generation. Far from trade being suspect precisely because it lacked disinterestedness, the new kind of highly interested economic activity is seen as the cornerstone of a new ethic. It takes the traditional ideals of the republic, liberty and equality, and plays them in a quite new register. Liberty is no longer simply belonging to the sovereign people, but personal independence. Moreover, this kind of liberty, generalized, is the necessary basis of equality, for it alone negates the older forms of hierarchical independence. What was seen in the old view as the source of self-centeredness, private interest, and corruption is now the driving force of a free and equal society.

Thus, the entrepreneur is seen as a benefactor. Narratives about such individuals, their rise from rags to riches, were recounted again and again, offering example and inspiration. In fact, the people who gained the greatest respect and admiration were those who both created new wealth and took leadership or contributed to public well-being; the paradigm was set for the successful entrepreneur-turned-benefactor, which has been so dominant in the United States ever since.[16]

Independence is thus a social, and not just a personal, ideal. It was valued as a contribution to national well-being and greatness and was correspondingly admired and lauded. By the same token, successful, enterprising individuals felt very much part of the larger society. They sought its admiration, praise, and confirmation; they competed for eminence and often took leadership roles.

Indeed, this revolution of personal independence heightened the sense of belonging to the wider society. It broke people out of narrower communities, but not to leave them in a kind of self-absorbed isolation. Rather, it allowed for a more intense sense of belonging to an impersonal society of equals. This was reflected, among other places, in the phenomenal growth of newspapers and periodicals and their circulation throughout the republic.[17] A society permeated by relations of personalized hierarchy had gone over fully to one based on impersonal equality.

Based on equality in theory, that is. Many people were still left out, not only in the niches still left untouched by the new principle, like the family in one way and the slave plantation in another. There was also in the self-congratulation around the new society a blindness toward the failures, the ones who didn't make it to riches, and even more toward the new forms of oppressive dependency arising in the growing factories, which employed largely marginal people, especially the new Irish immigrants. The crucial thing about America's development is that these people who couldn't make it to the celebratory family portrait of the enterprising never could find or erect the cultural space to unite around an alternative vision of the republic. The United States never, except perhaps briefly with Debs, had a serious socialist opposition.

I have been talking here of the American path that completes its long march, fully conscious of the fact that there are other national itineraries that pass through different sites and thus end up in a rather different place. The concept of social imaginaries perhaps allows us to come to grips with these national distinctions among otherwise similar North Atlantic liberal democracies. They arise in one sense from the different ways the original pathbreaking forms of the modern imaginary — economy, public sphere, and self-governing polity — ended up transforming the understanding of other levels and niches of social life. One of the crucial differences between the United States and many European societies lies in the fact that the spreading of the new political imaginary downward and outward took place on the Old Continent partly through the crystallization of a class imaginary of subordinate groups, particularly workers. This meant more than the sense of a common interest, among mechanics, for instance, present from the first days of the republic. The class imaginary of the British Labour movement or the French or German trade unions went beyond the sense that certain kinds of independent individuals shared an interest; it came closer to the sense of a common identity, shared within a local community (e.g., in mining villages in the UK) or the volonté générale of those who share a certain community of fate, as exploited workers, for instance. In some cases, it belonged to a political culture shaped by the Rousseauian redaction of the modern moral order, which was alien to the U.S. trajectory.

This suggests another way in which national cultures of democracy differ from each other. The historical trajectory, stretching way back, still colors the present understanding. We can see this if we refer back to the differences in political culture between the United States and France. I spoke there of how the new imaginary of popular sovereignty inherits some of its forms from the traditional political culture of the ancient constitution, in particular its forms of representation. But the new imaginary doesn't just displace the old one. It reinterprets the key values of the older tradition but retains the sense of its origin in this earlier tradition, and that precisely because the new was seen not as a break, but as a reinterpretation. So Americans go on seeing themselves as continuing an old tradition of freedom, even when they declare independence and go through the cultural revolution of the early nineteenth century. They go on referring to the Magna Charta even in the twentieth-first century. Similarly, Republican Frenchmen go on celebrating the taking of the

Bastille each July 14, even though they have long settled down in liberal modes of representative government. In each case, the present political culture is inflected by the past, both in what is revered in the national history and in what has been rejected.

Modern social imaginaries have been differently refracted in the divergent media of the respective national histories, even in the West. This warns us against expecting a simple repetition of Western forms when these imaginaries are imposed on or adopted in other civilizations.

have been describing our modern social imaginary in terms of the underlying idea of moral order, one that has captured in our characteristic social practices and forms the salient features of seventeenth-century natural law theory, while transforming this in the process. But it is clear that the change in the underlying notion of order has brought a number of other changes with it.

I have already mentioned the absence of an action-transcendent grounding, the fact that modern social forms exist exclusively in secular time. The modern social imaginary no longer sees the greater translocal entities as grounded in something other, something higher, than common action in secular time. This was not true of the premodern state, as I argued above. The hierarchical order of the kingdom was seen as based in the Great Chain of Being. The tribal unit was seen as constituted as such by its law, which went back since time out of mind, or perhaps to some founding moment that had the status of a "time of origins" in Eliade's sense. The importance in premodern revolutions, up to and including the English Civil War, of the backward look, of establishing an original law, comes from this sense that the political entity is action-transcendent. It cannot simply create itself by its own action; on the contrary, it can act as an entity because it is already constituted as such. That is why such legitimacy attaches to returning to the original constitution.

Seventeenth-century social contract theory, which sees a people as coming together out of a state of nature, obviously belongs to another order of thought. But, if my argument above is right, it wasn't until the late eighteenth century that this new way of conceiving things entered the social imaginary. The American Revolution is in a sense the watershed. It was undertaken in a backward-looking spirit, in the sense that the colonists were fighting for their established rights as **156** Englishmen. Moreover, they were fighting under their established colonial legislatures, associated in a Congress. But out of the whole process emerges the crucial fiction of "We, the people," into whose mouth the declaration of the new constitution is placed.

Here the idea is invoked that a people, or, as it was also called at the time, a "nation" can exist prior to and independently of its political constitution. So that this people can give itself its own constitution by its own free action in secular time. Of course, the epoch-making action rapidly comes to be invested with images drawn from older notions of higher time. The *Novus Ordo seclorum*, just like the new French revolutionary calendar, draws heavily on Judeo-Christian apocalypticism. The constitution founding comes to be invested with something of the force of a time of origins, a higher time, filled with agents of a superior kind, which we should ceaselessly try to reapproach. Nevertheless, a new way of conceiving things is abroad. Nations, people, can have a personality, can act together outside of any prior political ordering. One of the key premises of modern nationalism is in place, because without this, the demand for self-determination of nations would make no sense. This is the right for people to make their own constitution, unfettered by their historical political organization.

In order to see how this new idea of collective agency, the "nation" or "people," articulates into a new understanding of time, I want to return to Benedict Anderson's very insightful discussion. Anderson stresses how the new sense of belonging to a nation was prepared by a new way of grasping society under the category of simultaneity: society as the whole consisting of the simultaneous happening of all the myriad events that mark the lives of its members at that moment.[1] These events are the fillers of this segment of a kind of homogeneous time. This very clear, unambiguous concept of simultaneity belongs to an understanding of time as exclusively secular. As long as secular time is interwoven with various kinds of higher time, there is no guarantee that all events can be placed in unambiguous relations of simultaneity and succession. The high feast is in one way contemporaneous with my life and that of my fellow pilgrims, but in another way, it is close to eternity or the time of origins or the events it prefigures.

A purely secular time-understanding allows us to imagine society horizontally, unrelated to any "high points," where the ordinary sequence of events touches higher time, and therefore without recognizing any privileged persons or agencies, such as kings or priests, who stand and mediate at such alleged points. This radical horizontality is precisely what is implied in the direct-access society, where each member is "immediate to the whole." Anderson is undoubtedly right to argue that this new understanding couldn't have arisen without social developments like that of print capitalism, but he doesn't want to imply by this that the transformations of the social imaginary are sufficiently explained by these developments. Modern society required transformations also in the way we figure ourselves as societies. Crucial among these has been this ability to grasp society from a decentered view which is no one's. That is, the search for a truer and more authoritative perspective than my own doesn't lead me to center society on a king or sacred assembly or whatever, but allows for this lateral, horizontal view, which an unsituated observer might have: society as it might be laid out in a tableau without privileged nodal points. There is a close inner link among modern societies, their self-understandings, and modern synoptic modes of representation in "the Age of the World Picture":[2] society as simultaneous happenings, social interchange as impersonal system, the social terrain as what is mapped, historical culture as what shows up in museums, and so on.

There was thus a certain verticality of society, which depended on a grounding in higher time and which has disappeared in modern society. Seen from another angle, this was also a society of mediated access. In an ancien régime kingdom, such as France, the subjects are only held together within an order that coheres through its apex, in the person of the king, through whom this order connects to higher time and the order of things. We are members of this order through our relation to the king. As we saw in the previous chapter, earlier hierarchical societies tended to personalize relations of power and subordination.

The principle of a modern horizontal society is radically different. Each of us is equidistant from the center; we are immediate to the whole. This describes what we could call a direct-access society. We have moved from a hierarchical order of personalized links to an impersonal egalitarian one; from a vertical world of mediated access to horizontal, direct-access societies.

In the earlier form, hierarchy and mediacy of access went together. A society of ranks — "society of orders," to use Tocqueville's phrase — as in seventeenth-century France, was hierarchical in an obvious sense. But this also meant that one belonged to this society via belonging to some component of it. As a peasant, one was linked to a lord who in turn held from the king. One was a member of a municipal corporation which had a standing in the kingdom or exercised some function in a Parlement with its recognized status, and so on. By contrast, the modern notion of citizenship is direct. In whatever many ways I am related to the rest of society through intermediary organizations, I think of my citizenship as separate from all of these. My fundamental way of belonging to the state is not dependent on or mediated by any of these other belongings. I stand, alongside all my fellow citizens, in direct relationship to the state, which is the object of our common allegiance.

Of course, this doesn't necessarily change the way things get done. I know someone whose brother-in-law is a judge or an MP, and so I phone her up when I'm in a jam. We might say that what has changed is the normative picture. But underlying this, without which the new norm couldn't exist for us, is a change in the way people imagine belonging. There were certainly people in seventeenth-century France, and before, for whom the very idea of direct access would have been foreign, impossible to clearly grasp. The educated had the model of the ancient republic. But for many others, the only way they could understand belonging to a larger whole, like a kingdom or a universal church, was through the imbrication of more immediate, understandable units of belonging—parish, lord—into the greater entity. Modernity has involved, among other things, a revolution in our social imaginary, the relegation of these forms of mediacy to the margins and the diffusion of images of direct access.

This has come through the rise of the social forms I have been describing: the public sphere, in which people conceive themselves as participating directly in a nationwide (sometimes even international) discussion; market economies, in which all economic agents are seen as entering into contractual relations with others on an equal footing; and, of course, the modern citizenship state. But we can think of other ways as well in which immediacy of access takes hold of our imagination. We see ourselves in spaces of fashion, for instance, taking up and handing on styles; we see ourselves as part of the worldwide audience of media stars. And though these spaces are in their own sense hierarchical—they center on quasi-legendary figures—they offer all participants an access unmediated by any of their other allegiances or belongings. Something of the same kind, along with a more substantial mode of participation, is available in the various movements, social, political, religious, that are a crucial feature of modern life and that link people translocally and internationally into a single collective agency.

These modes of imagined direct access are linked to, indeed are just different facets of, modern equality and individualism. Directness of access abolishes the heterogeneity of hierarchical belonging. It makes us uniform, and that is one way of becoming equal. (Whether it is the only way is the fateful issue at stake in much of today's struggles over multiculturalism.) At the same time, the relegation of various mediations reduces their importance in our lives; the individual stands more and more free of them and hence has a growing self-consciousness as an individual. Modern individualism, as a moral idea, doesn't mean ceasing to belong at all—that's the individualism of anomie and breakdown—but imagining oneself as belonging to ever wider and more impersonal entities: the state, the movement, the community of humankind. This is the change that has been described from another angle as the shift from "network" or "relational" identities to "categorical" ones.[3]

We can see right away that, in an important sense, modern direct-access societies are more homogeneous than premodern ones. But this doesn't mean that there tends to be less de facto differentiation in culture and lifestyle between different strata than there was a few centuries ago, although this is undoubtedly true. It is also the case that the social imaginaries of different classes have come much closer together. It was a feature of hierarchical, mediated societies that the people in a local community, a village or parish, for instance, might have only the most hazy idea of the rest of their society. They would have some image of central authority, some mixture of good king and evil ministers, but very little notion of how to fill in the rest of the picture. In particular, their sense was rather vague of what other people and regions made up the kingdom. There was, in fact, a wide gap between the theory and social imaginary of political elites and that of the less educated classes or those in rural areas. This state of affairs lasted until comparatively recently in many countries. It has been well documented for France during most of the nineteenth century, in spite of the confident remarks of republican leaders about the nation "one and indivisible."[4] This split consciousness is quite incompatible with the existence of a direct-access society. The necessary transformation was ultimately wrought by the Third Republic, and the modern France theorized by the Revolution became real and all-embracing for the first time. This (in more than one sense) revolutionary change in the social imaginary is what Weber captures in his title *Peasants into Frenchmen*.

11 Agency and Objectification

Imagining ourselves in this horizontal, secular world involves our belonging to new kinds of collective agency, those grounded in common action in secular time. But at the other end of the spectrum, it also involves being able to grasp society as objectified, as a set of processes, detached from any agential perspective. I mentioned this double focus of modern consciousness of society in chapter 5. I would like to develop it somewhat here.

As long as society is seen as by its very nature cohering only as subject to the king or as ruled by its ancient law, because in each case this is what links our society to its grounding in higher time, it is hard to imagine it in any other terms or from any other angle. To see it just as a system, a set of connected processes, operating in partial independence from its political or legal or ecclesial ordering, requires this shift into pure secular time. It requires a perspective on society as a whole independent from the normative ordering that defines its coherence as a political entity. And this was well nigh impossible as long as a normative ordering embedded in higher time was seen as essentially defining the polity.

The first such independent take on society was that which grasped it as an economy, that is, as no longer just a particular domain of the management by the ruler of his kingdom, construed as an extended household, but as a connected system of transactions obeying its own laws. These laws apply to human actions as they concatenate, behind the backs of the agents; they constitute an invisible hand. We are at the antipodes of collective agency.

So the new horizontal world in secular time allows for two opposite ways of imagining society. On one side, we become capable of imagining new free, horizontal modes of collective agency, and hence of entering into and creating such agencies because they are now in our repertoire. On the other, we become capable of objectifying society as a system of norm-independent processes, in some ways analogous to those in nature. On the one hand, society is a field of common agency, on the other a terrain to be mapped, synoptically represented, analyzed, perhaps preparatory to being acted on from the outside by enlightened administrators.

We have become accustomed to experiencing these two perspectives as being in tension; we often fear that the first will be repressed or elided by the second, as our world comes more and more under bureaucratic management, which itself may turn out to be dominated by its own impersonal laws. But these two standpoints cannot be dissociated. They are coeval; they belong together to the same range of imaginings that derive from the modern moral order.

Central to this is the idea that the political is limited by the extrapolitical, by different domains of life that have their own integrity and purpose. These include but aren't exhausted by the economic. It is thus built in to the modern social imaginary that it allows us to conceive of society in extrapolitical forms, not just through the science that came to be called political economy, but also through the various facets of what we have come to call sociology. The very meaning of society in its modern sense points us to this entity which can be grasped and studied in various ways, of which the political is only one and not necessarily the most fundamental.

Our modern imaginary thus includes not only categories that enable common action, but also categories of process and classification that happen or have their effects behind the backs of the agents. We each can be placed in census categories in relation to ethnicity, language, income level, or entitlements in the welfare system, whether or not we are aware of where we fit or what consequences flow from this. And yet categories of both kinds, the active and the objective, can be essential to the social imaginary in the sense I've been using it here, that is, the ensemble of imaginings that enable our practices by making sense of them.

It is clear how the active do this: only if we understand ourselves as a collective agency can we have this kind of action in our repertoire. But the objective categories enable in another way. Grasping my society as an economy is precisely not grasping it as a collective action, but only because I understand the system in this way will I engage in market transactions the way I do. The system provides the environment my action needs to have the desired result, and I may want to assure myself from time to time that it is still working as intended (e.g., not heading into depression or hyperinflation).

Active and objective categories play complementary roles in our lives. It is close to inconceivable that we could dispense with the second. As for the symmetrical hypothesis—that we should have only objective imaginings of society, while our sense of agency should be entirely as individuals—this corresponds to one of the utopias (or dystopias) of the eighteenth century, that of enlightened despotism. The only agency allowed to affect the whole is the ruler, guided as he or she is by the best scientific understanding.

Only for fleeting moments did the political development of any society approximate to this, under the "enlightened" direction of Frederick II, Joseph II, Catherine the Great, and Pombal. It seems more than a mere accident that our history took a different direction. In a sense, it did so most strikingly through the development of the public sphere.

We can see here the complementarity at work. In a sense, the discussions in the public sphere depended on and consisted in the development of enlightened, objective understanding of society, economically, politically, juridically. Public opinion was seen from one perspective as ideally rational, the product of calm and reasoned discussion. But from another angle the public sphere was also inevitably seen as a common action. The discussion had an upshot: it crystallized into public opinion, a common mind or collective judgment. More fateful, this opinion became gradually but irresistibly a principle of legitimation.

Nothing is more striking than the emergence of this new force in the last twenty years of the ancien régime in France. Before 1770, enlightened opinion was seen as a potential nuisance or danger by the royal government. An attempt was made to control the circulation of ideas through censorship. As this came to be more and more obviously ineffective, some attempts were made to steer the public discussion through "inspired" interventions by friendly writers. By the time we get to the eve of the Revolution, public opinion comes to be seen as an irresistible force, forcing the king, for instance, to recall Necker, the finance minister whom he had earlier sacked.

Many things underlie this development, including the mounting uncontrolled debt of the government which put it at the mercy of its creditors. But an essential condition of the turnover was the growth of the common understanding itself, which underlay the very existence of such a thing as public opinion. A change in the social imaginary had brought a new political force onto the scene.

In a common contemporary image, public opinion was portrayed as a tribunal, a sort of supreme court that authority had to listen to. This was the tribunal Malesherbes praised as "independent of all powers and respected by all powers . . . that tribunal of the public . . . the sovereign judge of all the judges of the earth."[1] As Jacques Necker himself put it after the event in his history of the Revolution: "An authority has arisen that did not exist two hundred years ago, and which must necessarily be taken into account, the authority of public opinion."[2]

The modern social imaginary is thus both active and contemplative. It expands the repertoire of collective action, and also that of objective analysis. But it also exists in a range of intermediate forms. In speaking above about the typically modern, horizontal forms of social imaginary, in which people grasp themselves and great numbers of others as existing and acting simultaneously I mentioned the economy, the public sphere, and the sovereign people, but also the space of fashion. This is an example of a fourth structure of simultaneity. It is unlike the public sphere and the sovereign people, because these are sites of common action. In this respect, it is like the economy, where a host of individual actions concatenate behind our backs. But it is different from this as well, because our actions relate in the space of fashion in a particular way. I wear my own kind of hat, but in doing so, I am displaying my style to all of you, and in this, I am responding to your self-display, even as you will respond to mine. The space of fashion is one in which we sustain together a language of signs and meanings, which is constantly changing but which at any moment is the backgound needed to give our gestures the sense they have. If my hat can express my particular kind of cocky yet understated self-display, this is because of how the common language of style has evolved among us up to this point. My gesture can change it, and then your responding stylistic move will take its meaning from the new contour the language takes on.

The general structure I want to draw from this example of the space of fashion is that of a horizontal, simultaneous, mutual presence, which is not that of a common action, but rather of mutual display. It matters to each of us as we act that others are there, as witnesses of what we are doing and thus as codeterminers of the meaning of our action.

168

Spaces of this kind become more and more important in modern urban society, where large numbers of people rub shoulders, unknown to each other, without dealings with each other, and yet affecting each other, forming the inescapable context of each other's lives. As against the everyday rush to work in the Metro, where others can sink to the status of obstacles in my way, city life has developed other ways of being-with, for instance, as we each take our Sunday walk in the park or as we mingle at the summer street festival or in the stadium before the playoff game. Here each individual or small group acts on their own, but with the awareness that their display says something to others, will be responded to by them, will help build a common mood or tone that will color everyone's actions.

A host of urban monads hover on the boundary between solipsism and communication. My loud remarks and gestures are overtly addressed only to my immediate companions; my family group is sedately walking, engaged in our own Sunday outing; but all the time we are aware of this common space that we are building, in which the messages that cross take their meaning. This strange zone between loneliness and communication fascinated many of the early observers of this phenomenon as it arose in the nineteenth century. We can think of some of the paintings of Manet or of Baudelaire's avid interest in the urban scene, in the roles of flâneur and dandy, uniting observation and display.

Of course, these nineteenth-century urban spaces were topical; that is, all the participants were in the same place, in sight of each other. But twentieth-century communications have produced metatopical variants, when, for instance, we lob a stone at the soldiers before the cameras of CNN, knowing that this act will resonate around the world. The meaning of our participation in the event is shaped by the whole vast dispersed audience we share it with.

Just because these spaces hover between solitude and togetherness, they may sometimes flip over into common action; indeed, the moment they do so may be hard to pin-point. As we rise as one to cheer the crucial third-period goal, we have undoubtedly become a common agent, and we may try to prolong this when we leave the stadium by marching and chanting or even wreaking various forms of mayhem together. The cheering crowd at a rock festival is similarly fused. There is a heightened excitement at these moments of fusion, reminiscent of Carnival or of some of the great collective rituals of earlier days. So much so that some have seen these moments as among the new forms of religion in our world.[3] Durkheim gave an important place to these times of collective effervescence as founding moments of society and the sacred.[4] In any case, these moments seem to respond to some important felt need of today's "lonely crowd."

Some moments of this kind are, indeed, the closest analogues to the Carnival of previous centuries, as has frequently been noted. They can be powerful and moving, because they witness the birth of a new collective agent out of its formerly dispersed potential. They can be heady, exciting. But unlike Carnival, they are not enframed by any deeply entrenched if implicit common understanding of structure and counter-structure. They are often immensely riveting, but frequently also wild, up for grabs, capable of being taken over by a host of different moral vectors, either utopian revolutionary, xeno-phobic, or wildly destructive; or they can crystallize on some deeply felt, commonly cherished good, like ringing the key chains in Wenceslas Square or, as in the case of the funeral of Princess Diana, celebrating in an out-of-ordinary life the ordinary, fragile pursuit of love and happiness.

170   Remembering the history of the twentieth century, replete with the Nürnberg rallies and other such horrors, one has as much cause for fear as hope in these wild, kairotic moments. But the potentiality for them, and their immense appeal, is perhaps implicit in the experience of modern secular time.

I have dwelt at length on these ambiguous spaces of mutual display, but they obviously don't exhaust the range of possi-bilities between common action and objectification. There are also moments when a common space is filled with a power-ful shared emotion rather than an action, as with the millions of spectators watching the funeral of Diana. These vast meta-topical spectator spaces have become more and more impor-tant in our world.

Moreover, these different ways of being together don't just exist side by side. We have already seen how mutual dis-play, for instance, can sometimes flip over, at least momen-tarily, into common action. On a somewhat more enduring basis, what starts as a mere census category may be mobi-lized into common agency, making common demands, as with the unemployed or welfare recipients. Or previously existing agencies can lapse into mere passive categories. The modern

imaginary contains a whole gamut of forms in complex interaction and potential mutual transition.

This understanding of society as not just the polity, as having
many facets, has had another important impact in our world.
This consists in the sense that action in the political sphere
has to take account of the integrity of the other forms and
the goals people seek in them. It is true that the idea of politics as purely instrumental to, say, economic prosperity is
hotly contested in our world (and rightly so, I believe). In
fact, the emergence of popular sovereignty has given politics a new importance, which partly expressed itself in the
retrieval of forms and ideals from the ancient republics and
poleis, in which political activity stood at the apex of the citizen's life. But even so, the integrity of the other spheres cannot
be gainsaid. The drive to override them, to control all other
aspects of life in the name of some radiant future, has become familiar to us as the totalitarian temptation, visible early
on at the height of the Jacobin Terror and latterly in Soviet
communism and its offshoots. Not only do these attempts run
counter to certain fundamental features of our understanding
of moral order — most notably the demand for individual freedom and moral autonomy — but they themselves have generally been undertaken in the hope (vain, as it turns out) that
this hypercontrol would issue in a world of nonconstraint. For
Marxism, the ultimate end was the withering away of the state.
No more eloquent testimony is possible to the profound an-
choring of the prepolitical in our modern understanding as
the limit and goal of politics.

(In the case of the other great totalitarian temptation of
our century, fascism, we have, indeed, a frontal assault on our
understanding of moral order. This is one facet of the reaction
against this order, which I describe below. It is important to

see that this order has been and will continue to be contested. But it is hard to imagine its being replaced. We were lucky in that fascism was eliminated by military defeat in the first half of the century. But even if it hadn't suffered this fate, I doubt that fascist regimes could have indefinitely resisted the demands for greater freedom that are so anchored in our culture.)

This sense of the modern age as one that gives a crucial place to the nonpolitical was articulated early on by Benjamin Constant in his famous lecture on ancient and modern liberty.[5] The error of Jacobinism (and of Rousseau), according to Constant, was to think that the only freedom that matters to

us is that of political participation, which the ancients prized. But we have become people for whom economic prosperity and the satisfactions of private life also have a crucial importance. We cannot just apply the ancient models to our political life.

In order to give a fuller picture of our contemporary notions of moral order, we should add to the three forms of social existence we have already identified in our modern imaginary—economy, public sphere, and a polity ruled by the people—a fourth, which has been articulated in bills and charters of rights. Here is a crucial feature of the original Grotian-Lockean theory that has become embedded in our understanding of normative order. It has come to structure our social imaginary in somewhat the same way and by the same process as popular sovereignty has. That is, earlier practices were given a new sense, and thus came to be structured differently.

So just as the practices of getting consent from elected assemblies was transformed during the American Revolution into a new definition of political legitimacy, so, at the same time and through the same political changes, the practices embodying the primacy of law began to change their sense.

Instead of enshrining merely the rights of Englishmen, they began to be seen as reflections of the Natural Right, of which the great seventeenth-century theorists had spoken. These were invoked in the Declaration of Independence; the primacy of rights is given a further push by the first ten Amendments to the Constitution.

This whole development reaches its culmination in our time, in the period after the Second World War, in which the notion of rights as prior to and untouchable by political structures becomes widespread—although they are now called "human" rather than "natural" rights—and in which this consciousness is given expression in the entrenchment of charters of rights, by which ordinary legislation can be set aside when it violates these fundamental norms.

These declarations of rights are in a sense the clearest expression of our modern idea of a moral order underlying the political, which the political has to respect.

T he move to a horizontal, direct-access world, interwoven with an embedding in secular time, had to bring with it a different sense of our situation in time and space. It brings different understandings of history and modes of narration.

In particular, the new collective subject, a people or nation that can found its own state, that has no need for a previous action-transcendent foundation, needs new ways of telling its story. In some ways, these resemble the old stories of state founding, drawing on the old images of larger-than-life figures in a time of origins that we cannot recapture; think of some of the treatments of Washington and other Founders in American storytelling about their origins.

But for all the analogies, there is a clear difference. We are dealing with a story in purely secular time. The sense that the present, postfounding order is right has to be expressed in terms that consort with this understanding of time. We can no longer describe it as the emergence of a self-realizing order lodged in higher time. The category that is at home in secular time is rather that of growth, maturation, drawn from the organic realm. A potential within nature matures. So history can be understood, for instance, as the slow growth of a human capacity, reason, fighting against error and superstition. The founding comes when people arrive at a certain stage of rational understanding.

This new history has its nodal points, but they are organized around the stages of a maturing potential, that for reason or for rational control, for instance. In one story, our growth entails coming to see the right moral order, the interlocking relations of mutual benefit that we are meant to realize ("We hold these truths to be self-evident") on one hand; and achieving adequate self-control to put it into practice, on the other. When we are sufficiently advanced on both of these paths, we are at a nodal point, where a new and better society can be founded. Our founding heroes, for all their exceptional qualities, emerge out of a story of growth in secular time.

This can fit into the story (or myth) of progress, one of the most important modes of narration in modernity. But it can also fit into another widely invoked matrix, that of revolution. This is the nodal point of maturation in which people become capable of making a decisive break with age-old forms and structures that impede or distort the moral order. Suddenly, it becomes possible to carry out the demands of this order as never before. There is a heady sense that everything is possible, which is why the idea of revolution can easily turn into a powerful myth, that of a past nodal point whose infinite possibilities have been frustrated, betrayed, by treachery or pusillanimity. The revolution becomes something yet to be completed. This was a sustaining myth of the radical French Left during the nineteenth century and into the twentieth.[1]

But one of the most powerful narrative modes centers around the nation. There is something paradoxical about a people that can preside over its own political birth. What makes it that just these people belong together for purposes of self-rule? Sometimes, it is the accidents of history: a nation is born because the people who were hitherto ruled by a single authority decide to take this rule into their own hands (or certain elites decide that they have to be led to this end). This was the case in France in 1789 and, less happily, with the early twentieth-century attempts to establish an Ottoman nationality. Or else a people establishes itself out of the political choice for self-rule, as with the American Revolution. The revolutionaries separated themselves off from other Englishmen, even the Tories in their midst, by this decisive political option.

But much of what we call nationalism is based on the idea that there is some basis for the unit chosen other than historical contingency or political choice. The people being led to statehood is thought to belong together—in virtue of a common language, common culture, common religion, or history of common action. The point has been tirelessly made that much of this common past is frequently pure invention.[2] This is true, but it has certainly often been a politically effective invention, which has been interiorized and become part of the social imaginary of the people concerned.

Here again, the underlying category is that of growth of potential. In spite of our dispersion, multiplicity of dialects, lack of consciousness, we were an sich Ukrainians, Serbs, Slovaks, or whatever. We had important things in common that made it natural and right for us to function together as a single sovereign people. Only we needed to be awoken. Then, perhaps, we needed to struggle to realize this destiny. The idea of a maturation, a growth in consciousness, an an sich that ultimately becomes für sich, is central here.

These three modes of narrativity—progress, revolution, nation—can obviously be combined. And they can in turn be interwoven with apocalyptic and messianic modes drawn from religious understandings of *Heilsgeschichte* (history of salvation): for instance, the idea that the maturing order must confront violent opposition, the more violent the closer it is to ultimate victory. Revolution will be attended by a titanic struggle, a secularized Armageddon. The devastating effects of this in twentieth-century history have been all too evident.

Beyond this placing of our present in a national political history is our sense of our people's place in the whole epochal development or struggle for moral order, freedom, the right. This can be a very important part of our national self-understanding. Think of the place of a kind of universalist chauvinism in French national consciousness at the time of the French Revolution: France as the nation destined to bring freedom and the rights of man to Europe. Military glory and a universal mission are fused. This is heady stuff, as Napoleon knew. The USSR and communist China have tried to assume this mantle at different points in our century.

But there also is an extension of the imaginary in space. I have been talking of the nation or state as the locus for the three main forms of modern imaginary. But they all have supranational loci. The economy can be seen as international, and the public sphere always extended in some aspects beyond national borders; the exchange of ideas that was central to the European Enlightenment linked different national debates: English, Scottish, British, and later German and American. As for the European state itself, it has always existed within what was understood as a system of states, which reached a new stage of uniformity and a new set of ground rules with the peace of Westphalia in 1648.[3]

This sense of the unity of civilization goes way back, into the original self-understanding as Latin Christendom, bound together by an overarching supranational organization, the Catholic Church. Since then, under altered descriptions, of which the main modern one has been "Europe," this civilization has never lost the sense of its unity in shared principles of order.

If we now bring in civility or civilization in its other sense, not as a way of distinguishing one large cultural complex from another, but in the normative sense that contrasts with savagery or barbarism, we can say that in modern times, Europe has often seen itself not only or so much as Christendom, but as the main repository of civilization. And this sense of a supranational order has itself been gradually transformed over the centuries, until one of its principal defining characteristics has come to be democratic rule and respect for human rights. The modern moral order has colonized our understanding of this widest context of all. Since the European state system formed the basis of its extension into a world system, the order has been imaginatively expanded to include all the (properly behaved) members of the global community.

But this identification of civilization and the modern moral order didn't come about without opposition. A rearguard action was fought all the way on behalf of earlier monarchical-hierarchical models of order. From early on in the process these began to be affected by the modern notion of order, as we saw with the compromises implicit in the Baroque notion of order mentioned earlier. Revolutions could be followed by Restorations, but these never quite brought back the status quo ante, as Charles X discovered when he tried to stage a full-scale traditional coronation ceremony at Rheims in 1825. The ancient pageantry could no longer really come off in the new context. Other authoritarian regimes invested more in becoming *Machstaate* than they did in reviving forms of hierarchical complementarity. Some resorted to such bizarre and contradictory exercises as the appeal to a Russian nationalism mobilized under the tsar as autocrat.

Nevertheless these "reactionary" regimes fought a long rearguard battle and eventually handed the baton to twentieth-century forms of autocracy. There was some continuity of constituency between the two: some of those nostalgic for the order of Wilhelmine Germany joined the ranks of the Nazis; French fascists grew out of movements like Action Française, which was supposed to be seeking a monarchic restoration. But in fact, the two kinds of opposition to the modern moral order sprang from different sources. The twentieth-century opposition came from the reaction against this order, the continuing unease it has aroused since it first began to set the terms of politics in the eighteenth century.

We can see what this involves if we look at the unease that the advent of a polite commercial society aroused among many people in the eighteenth century. This modern society was more pacific, productive, and egalitarian than what had preceded it, and all these things were seen as good. But there was a nagging fear that something was lost in all this; that manliness, heroism, greatness of soul was being eroded; that the superiority of certain exceptional people was being drowned in the love of mediocrity.

Some of this sense of unease emerged in the continuing interest in republican virtue in the eighteenth century. Even some of those thinkers who gave us the most advanced and sophisticated theories of the new society and saw most clearly its advantages, for instance Adam Smith and Adam Ferguson, expressed a fear that a too great division of labor would stupefy and enervate, would unfit people to be self-ruling citizens, and would put an end to the courage and virtue of the warrior-citizen of yore. As Ferguson put it, "By separating the arts of the clothier and tanner, we are the better supplied with shoes and with cloth. But to separate the arts which form the citizen and the statesman, the arts of policy and war, is an attempt to dismember the human character." It would be to deprive a free people of what is necessary to its safety.[4]

This worry didn't die with the century. The nagging sense continually recurs that modern egalitarianism and the arts of peaceful production have been purchased at the expense of greatness, heroism, the courage to risk life, and the aspiration to something higher than prosperity. Tocqueville continually tempers his endorsement of democracy with the fear of a decline in freedom. And, of course, there was no greater critic of welfare and equality than Friedrich Nietzsche, with his contempt for the "pitiable comfort" sought by the "last men."

One remedy for this felt lack was to propose a more heroic and full-bodied search for equality in self-rule, of the kind Rousseau proposed. We see this with the Jacobins, with Marx, and with communism. The decline into a pitiable comfort is headed off by the heroic nature of the attempt to establish a new kind of republic of virtue, or a community of equal sharers. The other path followed Nietzsche in rejecting the egalitarian and humanitarian values of the modern order altogether, and proposed a new politics of heroism, domination, and the Will.

Both of these reactions produced totalitarian challenges to liberal democracy in the twentieth century, which came to define itself by a version of the modern moral order that stressed its plural forms and the limits of the political. It is the victories of liberal democracy in these struggles that seem finally to have entrenched the identity of civilization and the modern order. Although the sense of both communism and fascism as reacting against an established system seems to suggest that this identification was already well underway at the beginning of the century. Ezra Pound could speak of the tragically vain sacrifice of young men in the First World War:

> There died a myriad,
> And of the best, among them,
> For an old bitch gone in the teeth
> For a botched civilization.[5]

For the most part, we live now in Western societies with this identification utterly taken for granted—though we might be embarrassed by the politically incorrect invocation of civilization in a normative sense. We are both horrified by and (not always avowedly) look down on those who reject the basic values of this order, be they the terrorists of Al Qaeda or practitioners of genocide in the Balkans or Africa.

Moreover, we relate to this order as established in our civilization the way people have always related to their most fundamental sense of order: we have both a sense of security in believing that it is really in effect in our world and also a sense of our own superiority and goodness deriving from our participation in it and our upholding of it. This means that we can react with great insecurity when we see that it can be breached from outside, as at the World Trade Center; but also that we are even more shaken when we feel that it might be undermined from within or that we might be betraying it. There it is not only our security that is threatened; it is also our sense of our own integrity and goodness. To see this questioned is profoundly unsettling, ultimately threatening our ability to act.

This is why in earlier times, we see people lashing out at such moments of threat, scapegoating violence against "the enemy within," meeting the threat to our security by finessing that to our integrity, deflecting it onto the scapegoats. In earlier periods of Latin Christendom, Jews and witches were cast in this unenviable role. The evidence that we are still tempted to have recourse to similar mechanisms in our "enlightened" age is unsettling. But it would not be the first such paradox in history if a doctrine of peaceful universalism were invoked to mobilize scapegoating violence.[6]

This is the dark side of our modern Western social imaginary: its connections with our sense of civilizational superiority and its possible relation to the persecution of scapegoats. So, what is the relation of a social imaginary to what Marxists call ideology, a distorted or false consciousness of our situation? The very use of a term linked to imagination invites this question; what we imagine can be something new, constructive, opening new possibilities, or it can be purely fictitious, perhaps dangerously false.

In fact, my use of the term is meant to combine both these facets. Can an imaginary be false, meaning that it distorts or covers over certain crucial realities? Clearly, the answer to this is yes, in the light of some of the examples above. Take our sense of ourselves as equal citizens in a democratic state; to the extent that we not only understand this as a legitimat- ing principle but actually imagine it as integrally realized, we will be engaging in a cover-up, averting our gaze from various excluded and disempowered groups or imagining that their exclusion is their own doing. We regularly come across ways in which the modern social imaginaries, no longer defined as ideal types but as actually lived by this or that population, are full of ideological and false consciousness.

But the gain involved in identifying these social imaginaries is that they are never just ideology. They also have a constitutive function, that of making possible the practices that they make sense of and thus enable. In this sense, their falsity cannot be total; *some* people are engaging in a form of democratic self-rule, even if not everyone, as our comfortable self-legitimations imagine. Like all forms of human imagination, the social imaginary can be full of self-serving fiction and suppression, but it also is an essential constituent of the real. It cannot be reduced to an insubstantial dream.

E nough perhaps has been said to show how much our outlook is dominated by modes of social imaginary that emerge from what I have called the long march and has been shaped in one way or another by the modern ideal of order as mutual benefit. Not only the troubling aspects, like some forms of nationalism or purifying violence, but other, virtually unchallenged benchmarks of legitimacy in our contemporary world — liberty, equality, human rights, democracy — can demonstrate how strong a hold this modern order exercises on our social imaginary. It constitutes a horizon we are virtually incapable of thinking beyond. After a certain date, it is remarkable that even reactionaries can no longer invoke the older groundings in higher time. They too have to speak of the functional necessities of order, as with de Maistre's executioner. They may still think in theological terms, as do both de Maistre and Carl Schmitt (but, significantly, not Maurras). But this is theology in a quite different register. They have to speak as theorists of a profane world.[1]

What relation, then, does the modern social imaginary bear to modern secular society?

Well, plainly, as my use of the term secular implies, the long march must have contributed to a displacement of religion from the public sphere. It has helped to remove God from public space. Or so it might seem. But this is not quite true. It has certainly removed one mode in which God was formerly present, as part of a story of action-transcendent grounding of society in higher time. "The divinity that doth hedge a king" and the powerful range of analogies/assimilations between king and God, king and Christ, which Kantorowicz describes, are drastically undermined and finally dispelled by the imaginaries that have emerged from the order of mutual benefit.[2] But this doesn't mean that God must be altogether absent from public space. The American people who came to invoke itself as "we" also defined (define) itself as "one people under God." The order of mutual benefit was originally seen as God-created, and its fulfillment as God-destined.

In order to understand our present predicament, we have to see what this alternative form of God presence amounts to, and how it has been set aside in many contemporary societies.

The long march has plainly worked alongside and together with the forces that have carried us away from the enchanted cosmos shaped by higher times. There is, of course, a close connection between disenchantment and the confining of all action to profane time. The same factors that eventually dispel and empty the world of spirits and forces—worshipful living of ordinary life, mechanistic science, the disciplined reconstruction of social life—also confine us more and more to secular time. They empty and marginalize higher times, they repress the kairotic, multilevel time of Carnival, occlude the need for, even the possibility of, antistructure, and hence render notions of action-transcendent grounding less and less comprehensible. They plant us firmly in a secular time that is more and more mapped out and measured as a comprehensive environment without a chink that might give access to the former connections of higher time.

And so these latter disappear, albeit through a number of

transition stages, of which the great modes of Baroque public space are striking examples, as was also the Classicism of the Sun King.

Plainly, then, this social imaginary is the end of a certain kind of presence of religion or the divine in public space. It is the end of the era when political authority, as well as other metatopical common agencies, are inconceivable without reference to God or higher time, when these are so woven into the structures of authority that the latter cannot be understood separately from the divine, the higher, or the numinous. This is the step that Marcel Gauchet described as "the end of religion." But this alarming expression is given a more exact sense: it is the end of society as structured by its dependence on God or the beyond.[3] It is not the end of personal religion, as Gauchet insists.[4] It is not even necessarily the end of religion in public life, as the American case shows. However, it is undoubtedly a decisive stage in the development of our modern predicament, in which belief and unbelief can coexist as alternatives.

More precisely, the difference amounts to this. In the earlier phase, God or some kind of higher reality is an ontic necessity; that is, people cannot conceive a metatopical agency having authority that is not grounded somehow in higher time, be it through the action of God or the Great Chain or some founding *in illo tempore*. What emerges from the change is an understanding of social and political life entirely in secular time. Foundings are now seen to be common actions in profane time, ontically on the same footing with all other such actions, even though they may be given a specially authoritative status in our national narrative or our legal system.

This freeing of politics from its ontic dependence on religion is sometimes what people mean by the secularity of public space. There is no harm in this; indeed, it is probably a good idea to give it this sense. This is the picture of "le social fondé sur lui-même" (society as founded on itself), of which Baczko speaks.[5]

But we musn't lose from sight that this opens a new space for religion in public life. Regimes founded on common action in profane time are in a certain sense based on a common will. This doesn't mean that they are necessarily democratic; the common will may be that of a minority, it being taken for granted that they can speak for the rest or that the others are not capable of self-rule. The common will is even the grounding of fascist regimes, it being understood that the real will of the people is expressed through the Leader. In a sense, it is almost a tautology that, where we lose any ontic dependence on the higher and the polity emanates from some founding common action, the shared will that this action realizes is given a foundational role.

Of course, this reference to a common will is inescapable in democracies, which claim to be based on popular sovereignty. Here there is some common understanding of what the state is about, which provides the framework within which the ongoing deliberation can take place, the reference points of public discussion, without which periodic decisions cannot be recognized as expressions of the popular will. Because it is only if we have had a debate about a commonly identified issue, and one in which each of us has some chance at a hearing, that we will be able to recognize the outcome as a common decision.

More, if I am to accept as authoritative a decision that goes against me, I have to see myself as part of the people whose decision this is. I have to feel a bond with those who make up this people, such that I can say: Wrong as this decision is in its content, I have to go along with it as an expression of the will, or interest, of this people to whom I belong.

What can bond a people in this sense? Some strong common purpose or value. This is what I call their "political identity." Let me try to explain this further.

To take the case of democratic societies as our example, it is clear that this identity must involve freedom, and that must include the freedom of the dissenting minority. But can a decision that goes against me serve my freedom? Here we meet a long-standing skepticism, which is particularly strong among those who hold to an atomist political philosophy and who are suspicious of all appeals to a common good beyond individual choice. They see these appeals as just so much humbug to get contrary voters to accept voluntary servitude.

But we don't need to decide this ultimate philosophical issue here. We are dealing with a question not of philosophy, but of the social imaginary. We need to ask: What is the feature of our "imagined communities" by which people very often do readily accept that they are free under a democratic regime even where their will is overridden on important issues?

The answer they accept runs something like this: You, like the rest of us, are free just in virtue of the fact that we are ruling ourselves in common and not being ruled by some agency that need take no account of us. Your freedom consists in your having a guaranteed voice in the sovereign, that you can be heard and have some part in making the decision. You enjoy this freedom by virtue of a law that enfranchises all of us, and so we enjoy this together. Your freedom is realized and defended by this law, whether you win or lose in any particular decision. This law defines a community of those whose freedom it realizes/defends together. It defines a collective agency, a people, whose acting together by the law preserves their freedom.

Such is the answer, valid or not, that people have come to accept in democratic societies. We can see right away that it involves their accepting a kind of belonging much stronger than that of any chance group that might come together. It is an ongoing collective agency, membership in which realizes something very important: a kind of freedom. Insofar as this good is crucial to members' identity, they thus identify strongly with this agency, and hence also feel a bond with their coparticipants in this agency. It is only an appeal to this kind of membership that can answer the challenge of an individual or group who contemplates rebelling against an adverse decision in the name of their freedom.

The crucial point here is that, whoever is ultimately right philosophically, it is only insofar as people accept some such answer that the legitimacy principle of popular sovereignty can work to secure their consent. The principle is effective only via this appeal to a strong collective agency. If the identification with this is rejected, the rule of this government seems illegitimate in the eyes of the rejecters, as we see in countless cases with disaffected national minorities: rule by the people, all right; but we can't accept rule by this lot, because we aren't part of their people. This is the inner link between democracy and strong common agency. It follows the logic of the legitimacy principle that underlies democratic regimes. They fail to generate this identity at their peril.

This last example points to an important modulation of the appeal to popular sovereignty. In the version I just gave, the appeal was to what we might call "republican freedom." It is the one inspired by ancient republics and invoked in the American and French Revolutions. But very soon after, the same appeal began to take on a nationalist form. The attempts to spread the principles of the French Revolution through the force of French arms created a reaction in Germany, Italy, and elsewhere: the sense of not being part of, represented by that sovereign people in the name of which the Revolution was being made and defended. It came to be accepted in many circles that a sovereign people, to have the unity needed for collective agency, had already to have an antecedent unity, of culture, history, or (more often in Europe) language. And so behind the political nation, there had to stand a preexisting cultural (sometimes ethnic) nation.

Nationalism, in this sense, was born out of democracy, as a (benign or malign) growth. In early nineteenth-century Europe, as peoples struggled for emancipation from multinational despotic empires, joined in the Holy Alliance, there seemed to be no opposition between the two. For a Mazzini, they were perfectly converging goals.[6] Only later do certain forms of nationalism throw off the allegiance to human rights and democracy in the name of self-assertion.

But even before this stage, nationalism gives another modulation to popular sovereignty. The answer to the objecter above—something essential to your identity is bound up in our common laws—now refers not just to republican freedom, but also to something of the order of cultural identity. What is defended and realized in the national state is not just your freedom as a human being; this state also guarantees the expression of a common cultural identity.

We can speak therefore of a "republican" variant and a "national" variant of the appeal to popular sovereignty, though in practice the two often run together and often lie undistinguished in the rhetoric and imaginary of democratic societies.

(In fact, even the original republican prenationalist revolutions, the American and the French, have seen a kind of nationalism develop in the societies that issued from them. The point of these Revolutions was the universal good of freedom, whatever the mental exclusions that the revolutionaries in fact accepted, even cherished. But their patriotic allegiance was to the *particular historical project* of realizing freedom, in America, in France. The very universalism became the basis of a fierce national pride, in the "last, best hope for mankind," in the republic that was bearer of "the rights of man."

That's why freedom, at least in the French case, could become a project of conquest, with the fateful results in reactive nationalism elsewhere that I mentioned above.)

And so we have a new kind of collective agency, with which its members identify as the realization/bulwark of their freedom and the locus of their national/cultural expression. Of course, in premodern societies, too, people often "identified" with the regime, with sacred kings or hierarchical orders. They often were willing subjects. But in the democratic age, we identify as free agents. That is why the notion of popular will plays a crucial role in the legitimating idea.[7]

This means that the modern democratic state has generally accepted common purposes, or reference points, the features whereby it can lay claim to being the bulwark of freedom and locus of expression of its citizens. Whether or not these claims are actually founded, the state must be so imagined by its citizens if it is to be legitimate.

So a question can arise for the modern state for which there is no analogue in most premodern forms: What/whom is this state for? Whose freedom? Whose expression? The question seems to make no sense applied to, say, the Austrian or Turkish Empires, unless one answered the "whom for?" question by referring to the Habsburg or Ottoman dynasties, which would hardly give you their legitimating ideas.

This is the sense in which a modern state has a political identity, defined as the generally accepted answer to the What/whom for? question. This is distinct from the identities of its members, that is, the reference points, many and varied, which for each defines what is important in their lives. There better be some overlap, of course, if these members are to feel strongly identified with the state, but the identities of individuals and constituent groups will generally be richer and more complex, as well as being often quite different from each other.[8]

We can now see the space for religion in the modern state, for God can figure strongly in the political identity. It can be that we see ourselves as fulfilling God's will in setting up a polity that maximally follows his precepts, as many Americans have done in the revolutionary period and after. Or our national identity can refer to God, if we see ourselves as defined partly by our unique piety and faithfulness. This has often arisen among peoples who are surrounded, or worse, dominated by (what they see as) heretics and nonbelievers (e.g., the Afrikaners, Poles, Irish, French Canadians of yore). As they struggle to gain or preserve independence, a certain kind of fidelity to God, a certain confessional belonging becomes constitutive of their political identity. We have seen how this can later degenerate, so that the piety drains away and only the chauvinism remains, as in Northern Ireland and the former Yugoslavia, but this identity presence can also nourish a living faith.[9]

This is the new space for God in the secular world. Just as in personal life, the dissolution of the enchanted world can be compensated by devotion, a strong sense of the involvement of God in my life, so in the public world, the disappearance of an ontic dependence on something higher can be replaced by a strong presence of God in our political identity. In both individual and social life, the sacred is no longer encountered as an object among other objects, in a special place, time, or person. But God's will can still be very present to us in the design of things, in cosmos, state, and personal life. God can seem the inescapable source for our power to impart order to our lives, both individually and socially.

It was this shift from the enchanted to the identity form of presence that set the stage for the secularity of the contemporary world, in which God or religion is not precisely absent from public space, but is central to the personal identities of individuals or groups, and hence always a possible defining constituent of political identities. The wise decision may be to distinguish our political identity from any particular confessional allegiance, but this principle of separation has constantly to be interpreted afresh in its application, wherever religion is important in the lives of substantial bodies of citizens—which means virtually everywhere.[10] And the possibility is ever present of a reinvasion of the political identity by the confessional, as with the rise of the BJP in India.

Modernity is secular, not in the frequent, rather loose sense of the word, where it designates the absence of religion, but rather in the fact that religion occupies a different place, compatible with the sense that all social action takes place in profane time.

nd so secularity, as just defined, is another feature of Western modernity, another facet of the social imaginary that has helped to constitute this civilization. This brings us back to our starting point. I said at the outset that one of the principal possible gains from this study of our social imaginaries is that it is on this level that local particularities most clearly emerge.

If we define modernity in terms of certain institutional changes, such as the spread of the modern bureaucratic state, market economies, science, and technology, it is easy to go on nourishing the illusion that modernity is a single process destined to occur everywhere in the same forms, ultimately bringing convergence and uniformity to our world. Whereas my foundational hunch is that we have to speak of "multiple modernities," different ways of erecting and animating the institutional forms that are becoming inescapable, some of which I have just enumerated.

Nowhere does this hunch seem stronger than when we examine Western secularity, deeply marked as it is by the heritage of Latin Christendom, from which the word itself derives. But I hope that the point will now be more evident, at the end of this study, in a host of domains. Tracing the rise of the imaginary of popular sovereignty in the United States and France has brought out the differences in political culture even within the West (chapter 8), as do the different trajectories of the long march in the United States and Europe invoked in chapter 9. If we give its rightful place to the different understandings that animate similar institutions and practices even in the West, it should be all the more obvious how much greater are the differences among the major civilizations. The fact that these are in a sense growing closer to each other, and learning from each other, doesn't do away with but only masks the differences, because the understanding of what it is to borrow or to come close to the other is often very different from different standpoints.

With the realization that these differences matter comes the humbling insight that there is a lot that we don't understand, that we lack even the adequate language to describe these differences. Negatively, it is very important to set about "provincializing Europe," in Dipesh Chakrabarty's pithy phrase.[1] This means that we finally get over seeing modernity as a single process of which Europe is the paradigm, and that we understand the European model as the first, certainly, as the object of some creative imitation, naturally, but as, at the end of the day, one model among many, a province of the multiform world we hope (a little against hope) will emerge in order and peace. Then the real positive work, of building mutual understanding, can begin. For me, this process has begun at home, in describing the social imaginary of the modern West. But I hope that in a modest way it contributes to the larger project.

Notes

Introduction

1 Benedict Anderson, *Imagined Communities* (London: Verso, 1991).

1 The Modern Moral Order

1 In the *Second Treatise on Government*, John Locke defines the state of Nature as a condition "wherein all the Power and Jurisdiction is reciprocal, no one having more than another: there being nothing more evident, than that Creatures of the same species and rank promiscuously born to all the same advantages of Nature, and the use of the same faculties, should be equal one amongst another without Subordination or Subjection, unless the Lord and Master of them all, should by any manifest Declaration of his Will set one above another, and confer on him by evident and clear appointment an undoubted Right to Dominion and Sovereignty." See *Locke's Two Treatises of Government*, ed. Peter Laslett (Cambridge, England: Cambridge University Press, 1967), part 2, chap. 2, para. 4, p. 287.

2 See J. G. A. Pocock, *The Ancient Constitution and the Feudal Law*, 2d ed. (Cambridge, England: Cambridge University Press, 1987).

3 The term "moral economy" is borrowed from E. P. Thompson, "The Moral Economy of the English Crowd in the Eighteenth Century," *Past and Present* 50 (1971): 76–136.

4   *Macbeth*, 2.3.56; 2.4.17–18. See also Charles Taylor, *Sources of the Self* (Cambridge: Harvard University Press, 1992), 298.

5   Quoted in Louis Dupré, *Passage to Modernity* (New Haven: Yale University Press, 1993), 19.

6   "The sun will not overstep his measures; if he does, the Erinyes, the handmaids of Justice, will find him out." Quoted in George Sabine, *A History of Political Theory*, 3d ed. (New York: Holt, Rinehart and Winston, 1961), 26.

7   *Locke's Two Treatises*, part 1, chap. 9, para. 86, p. 223.

8   Ibid., part 2, chap. 2, para. 6, p. 289; see also part 2, chap. 11, para. 135, p. 376; and *Some Thoughts concerning Education*, para. 116.

9   *Locke's Two Treatises*, part 2, chap. 5, para. 34, p. 309.

10 See Eugen Weber, *Peasants into Frenchmen* (London: Chatto and Windus, 1979), chap. 28.

2   What Is a "Social Imaginary"?

1   See the discussions in Hubert Dreyfus, *Being in the World* (Cambridge: MIT Press, 1991) and John Searle, *The Construction of Social Reality* (New York: Free Press, 1995), drawing on the work of Heidegger, Wittgenstein, and Polanyi.

2   The way the social imaginary extends well beyond what has been (or even can be) theorized is illustrated in Francis Fukuyama's interesting discussion of the economics of social trust. Some economies find it difficult to build large-scale nonstate enterprises because a climate of trust that extends wider than the family is absent or weak. The social imaginary in these societies mark discriminations—between kin and nonkin—for purposes of economic association, which have gone largely unremarked in the theories of the economy that we all share, including the people in those societies. Governments can be induced to adopt policies, legal changes, incentives, and so on on the assumption that forming enterprises of any scale is there in the repertory and just needs encouragement. But the sense of a sharp boundary of mutual reliability around the family may severely restrict the repertory, however much it might be theoretically demonstrated to people that they would be better off changing their way of doing business. The implicit map of

social space has deep fissures, which are profoundly anchored in culture and imaginary, beyond the reach of correction by better theory. Francis Fukuyama, *Trust* (New York: Free Press, 1995).

3 Mikhail Bakhtin, *Speech Genres and Other Late Essays* (Austin: University of Texas Press, 1986).

4 This doesn't mean that utopias don't deal in their own kind of possibility. They may describe far-off lands or remote future societies that can't be imitated today, that we may never be able to imitate. But the underlying idea is that these things are really possible in the sense that they lie in the bent of human nature. This is what the narrator of More's book thinks: the Utopians are living according to nature. See Bronislaw Baczko, *Les Imaginaires Sociaux* (Paris: Payot, 1984), 75. This is also what Plato thought, who provided one of the models for More's book and for a host of other "utopian" writings.

5 Immanuel Kant, "Von dem Schematismus der reinen Verständnisbegriffe," in *Kritik der reinen Vernunft*, Berlin Academy Edition (Berlin: Walter de Gruyter, 1968), 3: 133–39.

3 The Specter of Idealism

1 See G. A. Cohen, *Karl Marx's Theory of History* (Oxford: Oxford University Press, 1979), on whose analysis I draw in the succeeding paragraphs.

2 This is the transition that Michael Mann, speaking of the English case, calls the move from the "coordinated to the organic state" (1: 458–63). He links it, in the context of the constitutional regimes of this period (England, Holland), to the creation of what he calls the "class-nation" (480). Michael Mann, *The Sources of Social Power* (Cambridge, England: Cambridge University Press, 1986).

3 This includes, but goes beyond, the important "monopoly of the legitimate use of physical force" of which Weber speaks. "Politics as a Vocation," H. H. Gerth and C. Wright Mills eds., *Max Weber* (New York: Oxford University Press, 1964), 78.

4 John Hale, *The Civilization of Europe in the Renaissance* (New York: Macmillan, 1993), 362. Spenser spoke of the "savage brutishness and (loathlie) fylthynes" of the Irish; see Anna Bryson, *From Courtesy to*

Civility (Oxford: Oxford University Press, 1998), 53. A common view was that "the base people [are] by nature uncivil, rude, untoward, discourteous, rough, savage, as it were barbarous" (quoted in Bryson, *From Courtesy to Civility, Civilization of Europe*, 64.

5   Hale, 367–68.

6   Ibid., 366. This term "polite" is, of course, another borrowing from the Greek term that "civil" translates.

7   Ibid., 367. See the statue of Charles V triumphing over savagery.

8   Ibid., 369–71.

9   See Montaigne, "Les Cannibales," in *Essais* (Paris: Garnier-Flammarion, 1969), book 1, chap. 31.

10 Justus Lipsius, *Six Bookes of Politickes*, trans. William Jones (London, 1594), 17; quoted in Hale, *Civilization of Europe*, 360.

11 This is the process that Bryson describes in her brilliant *From Courtesy to Civility*. I have learned a great deal from this book.

12 Quoted in ibid., 70.

13 Bryson also makes this point; see ibid., 72.

14 Henry Crosse, *Virtue's Commonwealth*; quoted in Michael Walzer, *The Revolution of the Saints* (Cambridge, MA: Harvard University Press, 1965), 208.

15 Quoted in Walzer, *Revolution of the Saints*, 211–12.

16 Dod and Cleaver, *Household Government*, sig. X3; quoted in ibid., 216.

17 Richard Baxter, *Holy Commonwealth* (London, 1659), 274; quoted in Walzer, *Revolution of the Saints*, 224.

18 See John Bossy, *Christianity in the West: 1400–1700* (Oxford: Oxford University Press, 1985), 40–41.

19 See Bronislaw Geremek, *La Potence ou la Pitié* (Paris: Gallimard, 1987), 35.

20 Ibid., 180.

21 Michel Foucault, *Histoire de la Folie à l'âge classique* (Paris: Gallimard, 1958).

22 Quoted in Peter Burke, *Popular Culture in Early Modern Europe* (Aldershot, England: Scholar, 1994), 209.

23 Quoted in ibid., 212.

24 Ibid., 217.

25 Of course, this didn't mean "police state" in the modern sense. *Polizei* (another term derived from polis) "had the connotation of administra-

tion in the broadest sense, that is, institutional means and procedures necessary to secure peaceful and orderly existence for the population of the land." Marc Raeff, *The Well-ordered Police State* (New Haven: Yale University Press, 1983), 5.

26 Ibid., 61, 86–87, 89.

27 Ibid., 87.

28 Ibid., 178.

29 Michel Foucault, *Surveiller et Punir* (Paris: Gallimard, 1975), part 3, chap. 1.

30 See J. A. G. Pocock, *The Machiavellian Moment* (Princeton: Princeton University Press, 1975).

31 See Philip Carter, *Men and the Emergence of Polite Society* (London: Longman, 2001), 25, 36–39.

32 See, e.g., Adam Ferguson, *An Essay on the History of Civil Society* (London: Transaction Books, 1980).

33 See Albert Hirschmann, *The Passions and the Interests* (Princeton: Princeton University Press, 1977).

34 See J. G. A. Pocock, *Barbarism and Religion* (Cambridge, England: Cambridge University Press, 1999); Karen O'Brien, *Narratives of Enlightenment* (Cambridge, England: Cambridge University Press, 1997); and Pierre Manent, *La Cité de l'Homme* (Paris: Fayard, 1994), part 1.

4 The Great Disembedding

1 See Robert Bellah, "Religious Evolution," in *Beyond Belief* (New York: Harper and Row, 1970), chap. 2.

2 Godfrey Lienhardt, *Divinity and Experience* (Oxford: Oxford University Press, 1961), 233–35.

3 Ibid., 292.

4 See, e.g., ibid., chap. 3; Roger Caillois, *L'Homme et le Sacré* (Paris: Gallimard, 1963), chap. 3.

5 This is a much discussed feature of aboriginal religion in Australia; see Lucien Lévy-Bruhl, *L'Expérience mystique et les Symboles chez les Primitifs* (Paris: Alcan, 1937), 180; Caillois, *L'Homme*, 143–45; W. E. H. Stanner, "On Aboriginal Religion," a series of six articles in *Oceania*, 30–33 (1959–63). The same connection to the land has been noted

with the Okanagan in British Columbia; see Jerry Mander and Edward Goldsmith, *The Case against the Global Economy* (San Francisco: Sierra Club Books, 1996), chap. 39.

6 John Stuart Mill, "On Liberty," in *Three Essays* (Oxford: Oxford University Press, 1975), 77.

7 See, e.g., S. N. Eisenstadt, ed., *The Origins and Diversity of Axial Age Civilizations* (Albany: State University of New York Press, 1986); Bellah, "Religious Evolution."

8 Karl Jaspers, *Vom Ursprung und Ziel der Geschichte* (Zürich: Artemis, 1949).

9 Stanner, "On Aboriginal Religion," *Oceania* 30, no. 4 (June 1960): 276. See also by the same author "The Dreaming," in W. Lessa and E. Z. Vogt, eds., *Reader in Comparative Religion* (Evanston, IL: Row, Peterson, 1958), 158–67.

10 Stanner, "On Aboriginal Religion," *Oceania* 33, no. 4 (June 1963): 269.

11 I have been greatly helped here by the much richer account of religious development in Bellah's "Religious Evolution." My contrast is much simpler than the series of stages Bellah identifies; the primitive and the archaic are fused in my category of early religion. My point is to bring into sharp relief the disembedding thrust of the axial formulations.

12 See Marcel Gauchet, *Le désenchantement du monde* (Paris: Gallimard, 1985), chap. 2.

13 Louis Dumont, "De l'individu-hors-du-monde à l'individu-dans-le-monde," in *Essais sur l'individualisme* (Paris: Seuil, 1983).

14 See Fukuyama, *Trust*.

15 Ivan Ilich, *The Corruption of Christianity* (Toronto: Canadian Broadcasting Corporation, Ideas series, January 2000).

16 See René Girard, *Je vois Satan tomber comme l'éclair* (Paris: Grasset, 1999).

5 The Economy as Objectified Reality

1 Leslie Stephen, *History of English Thought in the 18th Century* (Bristol, England: Thoemmes, 1997), 2: 72.

2 *Mémoires*, 63, quoted in Nanerl Keohane, *Philosophy and the State in France* (Princeton: Princeton University Press, 1980), 248.

3   Keohane, *Philosophy*, 249–51.

4   Of course, a large and complex thesis lies behind this flip reference. The basic idea is that Baroque culture is a kind of synthesis of the modern understanding of agency as inward and poiêtic, constructing orders in the world, and the older understanding of the world as cosmos, shaped by Form. With hindsight, we tend to see the synthesis as instable, as doomed to be superseded, as it was in fact.

But whatever the truth of this, we can see in Baroque culture a kind of constitutive tension between an order already there and hierarchical, and agents who continue and complete it through their constructive activity and hence tend to understand themselves as acting out of themselves, and thus in this respect as situated outside of hierarchy and thus equal. Hence hybrid formulations such as those of Louis XIV.

I have learned much from the very interesting description of Baroque art in Dupré's *Passage to Modernity*, 237–48. Dupré speaks of the Baroque as the "last comprehensive synthesis" between human agency and the world in which it takes place, where the meanings generated by this agency can find some relation to those we discover in the world. But it is a synthesis filled with tension and conflict.

Baroque churches focus this tension not so much on the cosmos as static order, but on God, whose power and goodness is expressed in the cosmos. But this descending power is taken up and carried forward by human agency, creating "the modern tension between a divine and a human order conceived as separate centres of power" (226).

Baroque culture, Dupré argues, is united by "a comprehensive spiritual vision. . . . At the centre of it stands the person, confident in the ability to give form and structure to a nascent world. But—and here lies its religious significance—that centre remains vertically linked to a transcendent source from which, via a descending scale of mediating bodies, the human creator draws his power. This dual centre—human and divine—distinguishes the Baroque world picture from the vertical one of the Middle Ages, in which reality descends from a single transcendent point, as well as from the unproblematically horizontal one of later modernity, prefigured in some features of the Renaissance. The tension between the two centres conveys to the Baroque a complex, restless, and dynamic quality" (237).

5   Keohane, *Philosophy*, 164–67.

6   I have discussed this at greater length in Charles Taylor, *Sources of the Self* (Cambridge, MA: Harvard University Press, 1989), chap. 13.

7   Hirschmann, *The Passions and the Interests*. I am greatly indebted to the discussion in this extremely interesting book.

8   Alexander Pope, *Essay on Man*, part 3, 9–26, 109–14; part 4, 396.

9   See the interesting discussion in Mary Poovey, *A History of the Modern Fact* (Chicago: University of Chicago Press, 1998), chap. 3.

10 See J. B. Schneewind, *The Invention of Autonomy* (Cambridge, England: Cambridge University Press, 1998), part 1; Manent, *La Cité de l'Homme*, part 1.

11 Carter, *Men and the Emergence of Polite Society*, chaps. 3, 4; Bryson, *From Courtesy to Civility*, chap. 7.

12 Indeed, what we now consider the heights of Enlightenment social science, from Montesquieu to Ferguson, was not monochrome; these writers drew not only on the modern mode of objectifying science, but also on the traditional republican understanding. Adam Smith not only formulated the invisible hand, he also pondered the negative consequences of the extreme division of labor for citizenship and martial spirit "of the great body of the people." Adam Smith, *The Wealth of Nations* (Oxford: Clarendon Press, 1976), 2: 787. Ferguson, the author of one of the most influential stadial theories of commercial society, studied the conditions in which such societies could succumb to corruption. Adam Ferguson, *Essay on the History of Civil Society* (New Brunswick, NJ: Transaction Books, 1980), parts 5, 6.

6 The Public Sphere

1   Jürgen Habermas, *The Structural Transformation of the Public Sphere*, trans. Thomas Burger (Cambridge, MA: MIT Press, 1989); German original: *Strukturwandel der Öffentlichkeit* (Neuwied: Luchterhand, 1962); Michael Warner, *The Letters of the Republic* (Cambridge, MA: Harvard University Press, 1990).

2   Warner, *Letters*, chap. 1.

3   This indicates how far the late eighteenth-century notion of public opinion is from the object of poll research today. The phenomenon that public opinion research aims to measure is, in terms of my dis-

tinction, a convergent unity and doesn't need to emerge from discussion. It is analogous to the opinion of mankind. The ideal underlying the eighteenth-century version emerges in this passage from Burke, quoted by Habermas (*Structural Transformation*, 117–18): "In a free country, every man thinks he has a concern in all public matters; that he has a right to form and deliver an opinion on them. They sift, examine and discuss them. They are curious, eager, attentive and jealous; and by making such matters the daily subjects of their thoughts and discoveries, vast numbers contract a very tolerable knowledge of them, and some a very considerable one. . . . Whereas in other countries none but men whose office calls them to it having much care or thought about public affairs, and not daring to try the force of their opinions with one another, ability of this sort is extremely rare in any station of life. In free countries, there is often found more real public wisdom and sagacity in shops and manufactories than in cabinets of princes in countries where none dares to have an opinion until he comes to them."

4 Habermas, *Structural Transformation*, 119.

5 Warner, *Letters*, 41.

6 See Fox's speech, quoted in Habermas, *Structural Transformation*, 65–66: "It is certainly right and prudent to consult the public opinion. . . . If the public opinion did not happen to square with mine; if, after pointing out to them the danger, they did not see it in the same light with me, or if they conceived that another remedy was preferable to mine, I should consider it as my due to my king, due to my Country, due to my honour to retire, that they might pursue the plan which they thought better, by a fit instrument, that is by a man who thought with them. . . . But one thing is most clear, that I ought to give the public the means of forming an opinion."

7 Quoted in Habermas, *Structural Transformation*, 117.

8 Ibid., 82.

9 See Warner, *Letters*, 40–42. Warner also points to the relationship with the impersonal agency of modern capitalism (62–63), as well as the closeness of fit between the impersonal stance and the battle against imperial corruption, which was so central a theme in the colonies (65–66), in the framing of this highly overdetermined mode.

10   Ibid., 46.

11   See E. Kantorowicz, *The King's Two Bodies* (Princeton: Princeton University Press, 1957).

12   For an extra-European example of this kind of thing, see Clifford Geertz's *Negara* (Princeton: Princeton University Press, 1980), where the pre-Conquest Balinese state is described.

13   I describe this picture of premodern time consciousness, involving different modes of higher time, in Charles Taylor "Die Modernitaet und die saekulare Zeit," in Krzysztof Michalski, ed., *Am Ende des Milleniums: Zeit und Modernitaeten* (Stuttgart: Klett Kotta, 2000), 28–85.

14   As a matter of fact, excluding the religious dimension is not even a necessary condition of my concept of secular let alone a sufficient one. A secular association is one grounded purely on common action, which excludes any divine grounding *for this association*, but nothing prevents the people so associated from continuing a religious form of life; indeed, this form may even require that, for example, political associations be purely secular. There are, for instance, *religious* motives for espousing a separation of church and state.

15   Mircea Eliade, *The Sacred and the Profane* (New York: Harper, 1959), 80.

16   In *Imagined Communities*, Anderson borrows a term from Benjamin to describe modern profane time. He sees it as a "homogeneous, empty time." Homogeneity captures the aspect I am describing, that all events now fall into the same kind of time. But the "emptiness" of time takes us into another issue: the way in which both space and time come to be seen as "containers" that things and events contingently fill, rather than as constituted by what fills them. This latter step is part of the metaphysical imagination of modern physics, as we can see with Newton. But it is the step to homogeneity that is crucial for secularization, as I am conceiving it.

    The step to emptiness is part of the objectification of time that has been so important a part of the outlook of the modern subject of instrumental reason. In a sense, time has been "spatialized." Heidegger mounted a strong attack on this whole conception in his understanding of temporality; see especially *Sein und Zeit* (Tübingen: Niemeyer,

1926), division 2. But distinguishing secularity from the objectification of time allows us to situate Heidegger on the modern side of the divide. Heideggerian temporality is also a mode of secular time.

7 Public and Private

1   Habermas, *Structural Transformation*, chap. 2, sections 6 and 7.
2   See Taylor, *Sources of the Self*, chap. 13.
3   In the discussion that follows, I have drawn lavishly on the insightful analysis of Jeff Weintraub, "The Theory and Politics of the Public/Private Distinction," in Jeff Weintraub and Krishan Kumar, eds., *Public and Private in Thought and Practice* (Chicago: University of Chicago Press, 1997), 1–42.
4   Francis Fukuyama, whose discussion of this point in *Trust* I found very helpful, also holds that the new sociability that arises from this strand of the Reformation helped to create the conditions for a very successful mode of capitalist development.

8 The Sovereign People

1   This was not as big a step as it might seem, because in the understanding of the colonists, the rights they enjoyed as Britons were already seen as concrete specifications of "natural" rights; see Bernard Bailyn, *The Ideological Origins of the American Revolution* (Cambridge, MA: Harvard University Press, 1992), 77–78, 187–188.
2   "Nul ne craint aux Étas-Unis, comme c'est le cas en France, que le rapport de délégation puisse être assimilé à une pure forme de domination." Pierre Rosanvallon, *La Démocratie inachevée* (Paris: Gallimard, 2000), 28. This profound agreement on forms of representation didn't obviate very vigorous debates on structures, as we can see in the raging controversies around the new federal Constitution. It even allowed some profound issues to be raised about the nature of representation; see Bailyn, *The Ideological Origins of the American Revolution*, chap. 5. Nor did this basic agreement prevent popular uprisings against laws voted by assemblies, as with Shay's rebellion. The point was that these rebellions were not attempting to set up rival modes of legitimacy; they

were, rather, the last resort against what were seen as crying injustices that a system, however legitimate, could still enact. In this, they were rather analogous to the uprisings in ancien régime France, discussed below. See the interesting treatment in Patrice Gueniffey, *La Politique de la Terreur* (Paris: Fayard, 2000), 53–57.

3   François Furet, *La Révolution Française* (Paris: Hachette, 1988).

4   See Simon Schama, *Citizens* (New York: Knopf, 1989), chap. 4.

5   Orlando Figes, *A People's Tragedy* (London: Penguin, 1997), 98–101, 518–19.

6   Locke had already developed an embryonic form of this mechanism. In his chapter on property, he assures us, "He who appropriates land to himself by his labour, does not lessen but increase the stock of mankind. For the provisions serving to the support of humane life, pro-

208   duced by one acre of inclosed and cultivated land, are (to speak much within compasse) ten times more, than those, which are yielded by an acre of Land, of an equal richnesse, lying wast in common. And therefore he, that incloses Land and has a greater plenty of the conveniencys of life from ten acres, than he could have had from an hundred left to Nature, may truly be said, to give ninety acres to Mankind" (*Second Treatise of Civil Government*, 5.37).

7   J.-J. Rosseau, *Du Contrat Social*, book 1, chap. 6.

8   Ibid., book 1, chap. 8.

9   Ibid.

10 J.-J. Rousseau, "Profession de foi du vicaire savoyard," in *Émile* (Paris: Éditions Garnier, 1964), 354–55.

11 Quoted in Georges Lefebvre, *Quatre-Vingts-neuf* (Paris: Éditions Sociales, 1970), 245–46.

12 Montesquieu, *L'Esprit des Lois*, book 4, chap. 5.

13 François Furet, *Penser la Révolution française* (Paris: Gallimard, 1978), 276.

14 Jean Starobinski, *Jean-Jacques Rousseau: La Transparence et l'Obstacle* (Paris: Gallimard, 1971).

15 J.-J. Rousseau, *Lettre à d'Alembert sur les spectacles*, in *Du Contrat Social* (Paris: Classiques Garnier, 1962), 225. We can see from this how the transparency that Rousseau seeks is the enemy of representation in all its forms, whether political, theatrical, or linguistic. For certain

two-place relations, transparency and unity demand that the same term figure in both places. These include the relation x governs y, as well as x portrays something before y.

16 Mona Ozouf, *La fête révolutionnaire* (Paris: Gallimard, 1976).

17 Gueniffey, *La Politique*, makes good use of this distinction in his discussion.

18 Furet, *Penser*, 271.

19 Just how elaborate and (to us) horrifying these could be one can glean from the description of the execution of Damiens, who made an attempt on the life of Louis XV in 1757, in the riveting opening pages of Foucault's *Surveiller et Punir*.

20 Gueniffey makes the point that the ancien régime popular insurrection "n'exprime aucune revendication sur le pouvoir, mais équivaut au contraire à une reconnaissance implicite de l'autonomie de ce dernier. . . . Le peuple revendique moins la souveraineté qu'il n'affirme son droit de n'être pas opprimé" (*La Politique*, 78–79).

21 Albert Soboul, "Violences collectives et rapports sociaux: Les foules révolutionnaires (1789–95)," in *La Révolution française* (Paris: Gallimard, 1981), 578.

22 William Sewell, "Historical Events as Transformations of Structure: Inventing Revolution at the Bastille," *Theory and Society* 25 (1996): 841–81.

23 Colin Lucas, "The Crowd and Politics," in Colin Lucas, ed., *The Political Culture of the French Revolution* (Oxford: Pergamon Press, 1988), 259–85, traces the changes that the Revolution introduced in the practice of urban crowds. It would appear that the reinterpretation that the elites were proposing had some effect. For one thing, the demands they made began to go beyond the merely particular; they began to include certain larger political objectives. "Vive la nation! Le blé va diminuer!" chanted the crowd at Nogent-le-Rotrou, allying traditional demands to the new agenda of national politics (276). And the crowd that invaded the Convention in Germinal-Prairial of year 3 called for "du pain et la Constitution de 1793" (278). Linked to this enlargement of its objectives, crowds were now sometimes ready to be mobilized by the militants of the revolutionary clubs, that is, people outside their usual range of leaders. This was the formula for the famous journées.

On the other hand, the crowds still seemed to take for granted that normal power resided elsewhere; they waited for the duly constituted authorities to take their responsibilities. Even those who invaded the Convention in 1795 didn't know what to do once they had entered the premises; they deferred to the leadership of radical deputies.

24 Thompson, "The Moral Economy of the English Crowd in the Eighteenth Century," 76–136.

25 Foucault, *Surveiller et Punir*.

26 Soboul, "Violences collectives et rapports sociaux," 577.

27 Ibid., 579. Soboul also remarks on how much collective actions were aimed at precise goals and took for granted a certain traditional morality: "Le pillage répondait à l'égalitarisme foncier des sans-culottes: la reprise individuelle se légitimait par la disproportion des conditions d'existence, l'exhortation au pillage ou son apologie n'ayant jamais d'ailleurs visé que les boutiques de comestibles et de denrées de première nécessité" (578). In addition, there was a certain proportionality in the rate of reprisals, stretching from hanging in effigy right up to the supreme penalty.

28 See François Furet, *La Révolution française au débat* (Paris: Gallimard, 1999).

29 Quoted in Soboul, *La Révolution française*, 289. Gueniffey shows how this influence of the Parisian crowds, with their obsessions about enemies and plots, cleverly stirred up by Marat and others, began very early to alter the liberal convictions of the members of the Constituent Assembly. For some of them, it seemed necessary to make a semblance at least of doing what the populace demanded. One had to appease "la fermentation populaire," create an "abcès de fixation" for extraparliamentary agitation, "faire obstacle au déchaînement d'une violence ressentie comme barbare et primitive" (*La Politique*, 81–93).

30 See Lucas, "The Crowd and Politics," 259–85.

31 Robespierre's extravagant metaphysicopolitical ambitions in the last months of his reign are laid out in the report he made to the Convention on 5 February 1794: the aim of the Revolution was to vanquish vice and inaugurate a reign of virtue, in order to "remplir les voeux de la nature, accomplir les destinées de l'humanité, tenir les promesses de la philosophie, absoudre la Providence du long règne du crime et de

la tyrannie," by substituting "toutes les vertus et tous les miracles de la république à tous les vices et tous les ridicules de la monarchie" (quoted in Gueniffey, *La Politique*, 313).

32 This whole link between Revolution and violence needs further study, preferably with the aid of the writings of René Girard. I have discussed the social imaginaries of the French Revolution and their relation to the Terror at somewhat greater length in Charles Taylor, "La Terreur et l'imaginaire moderne," François Furet memorial lecture, May 2001. But this just scratches the surface of the immense problem of modern, postrevolutionary violence.

33 Furet, *Penser la Révolution française*.

34 Pierre Rosanvallon, *Le Moment Guizot* (Paris: Gallimard, 1985), 16–17, 285.

35 Robert Tombs, *France: 1814–1914* (London: Longman, 1996), 20–26. **211**

36 Rosanvallon, *Le Moment Guizot*, 80, chap. 9.

37 "Je parle pour ceux qui, parmi les conservateurs, ont quelque souci de la stabilité, quelque souci de la légalité, quelque souci de la modération pratiquée avec persévérance dans la vie publique. Je leur dis, à ceux-là: comment ne voyez-vous pas qu'avec le suffrage universel, si on le laisse librement fonctionner si on respecte, quand il s'est prononcé, son indépendance et l'autorité de ses décisions, comment ne voyez-vous pas, dis-je, que vous avez là un moyen de terminer pacifiquement tous les conflits, de dénouer toutes les crises, et que, si le suffrage universel fonctionne dans la plénitude de la souveraineté, il n'y a pas de révolution possible, parce qu'il n'y a plus de révolution à tenter, plus de coup d'État à redouter quand la France a parlé." Gambetta's speech of 9 October 1877, quoted in Rosanvallon, *Le Moment Guizot*, 364–65.

38 Pierre Rosanvallon, *Le Sacre du Citoyen* (Paris: Gallimard, 1992).

9 An All-Pervasive Order

1 E. S. Morgan, *Inventing the People* (New York: Norton, 1988).

2 Quoted in Gordon Wood, *The Radicalism of the American Revolution* (New York: Vintage, 1993), 43–44.

3 "L'aristocratie avait fait de tous les citoyens une longue chaîne qui remontait du paysan au roi; la démocratie brise la chaîne et met chaque

anneau à part." Alexis de Tocqueville, *La Démocratie en Amérique* (Paris: Garnier-Flammarion, 1981), 2: 126.

4 See, for instance, Locke, *Second Treatise of Government*, chap. 6, para. 75: "But these two Powers, Political and Paternal, are so perfectly distinct and separate; are built upon so different Foundations, and given to so different ends," (*Locke's Two Treatises*, 332).

5 Indeed, in our contemporary, "advanced," Western liberal societies, there are always important minorities in the population who continue to see their family or religious life, for instance, as operating on a quite different model from that larger political and economic system. This is often true of recent immigrants, for example.

6 I have drawn here on Wood, *The Radicalism of the American Revolution*, and Joyce Appleby, *Inheriting the Revolution* (Cambridge, MA: Harvard University Press, 2000); see also Bailyn, *The Ideological Origins of the American Revolution*.

7 Wood, *Radicalism*, 197.

8 Ibid., 95–109.

9 Ibid., 311.

10 Tocqueville, *La Démocratie en Amérique*, vol. 2, part 2, chap. 2; 125.

11 Appleby, *Inheriting*, 11.

12 Ibid., 201.

13 Ibid., 206, 215.

14 See David Martin, *Tongues of Fire* (Oxford: Blackwell, 1990). This is not just a phenomenon visible in evangelical Christianity. One could argue, for instance, that conversion to the Nation of Islam was the occasion of a similar empowerment for many African Americans.

15 Appleby, *Inheriting*, 145.

16 Ibid., 123–24, 257–58.

17 Ibid., 99–103.

10 The Direct-Access Society

1 Anderson, *Imagined Communities*, 37.

2 Martin Heidegger, "Die Zeit des Weltlbildes," in *Holzwege* (Frankfurt: Niemeyer, 1972).

3 I have borrowed this terminology from Craig Calhoun; see, e.g., "Nationalism and Ethnicity," *American Review of Sociology*, no. 9 (1993):

230. The discussion in this section owes a great deal to Calhoun's recent work.

4 This has been admirably traced by Weber, *Peasants into Frenchmen* (London: Chatto, 1979).

11 Agency and Objectification

1 Quoted in Keith Baker, *Inventing the French Revolution* (Cambridge, England: Cambridge University Press, 1990), 189.

2 Quoted in Stephen Holmes, *Benjamin Constant and the Making of Modern Liberalism* (New Haven: Yale University Press, 1985), 243.

3 See Danièle Hervieu-Léger, *La Religion pour Mémoire* (Paris: Cerf, 1993), chap. 3, especially 82.

4 Émile Durkheim, *Les Formes élémentaires de la Vie religieuse* (Paris: Presses Universitaires de France, 1912).

5 Benjamin Constant, "De la liberté des anciens, comparée à celle des modernes," in Marcel Gauchet, ed., *Écrits Politiques* (Paris: Gallimard, 1997).

12 Modes of Narration

1 Baczko, *Les Imaginaires Sociaux*, 117–18. I have drawn a great deal on the interesting discussions in this book.

2 See Ernest Gellner, *Nations and Nationalism* (Oxford: Blackwell, 1983); Eric Hobsbawm, *Nations and Nationalism since 1780* (Cambridge, England: Cambridge University Press, 1990).

3 Michael Mann, in his *Sources of Social Power*, makes the point very strongly that Western Europe always had an understanding of a supranational order in which individual states functioned.

4 Ferguson, *Essay on the History of Civil Society*, 230. This unease also underlies the sense among the Republican leaders of the American Revolution that ordinary people, engaged in making the means to life, couldn't rise to disinterested virtue, and that those engaged in trade would have trouble doing this too.

5 From Ezra Pound, *Hugh Selwyn Mauberley*, quoted in Samuel Hynes, *A War Imagined* (London: Pimlico, 1990), 342.

6 This whole issue of violence in modernity deserves further extensive

treatment, especially taking account of the pathbreaking work of René Girard.

13 The Meaning of Secularity

1   The pathos involved in the attempt to recover the unrecoverable was well illustrated by Charles X's attempt to restore the whole original liturgy in his coronation at Rheims in 1825. See the description in Furet, *Revolutionary France*, 300–303.

2   Kantorowicz, *The King's Two Bodies*.

3   "La fin du rôle de structuration de l'espace social que le principe de dépendance a rempli dans l'ensemble des sociétés jusqu'à la nôtre" (Gauchet, *Le désenchantement du monde*, 233). I have learned a great deal from this fascinating and profound work.

4   Ibid., 292.

5   Baczko, *Les Imaginaires Sociaux*, 17.

6   In fact, the drive to democracy took a predominantly "national" form. Logically, it is perfectly possible that the democratic challenge to a multinational authoritarian regime (e.g., Austria, Turkey) should take the form of a multinational citizenship in a pan-imperial "people." But in fact, attempts at this usually fail, and the people take their own road into freedom. So the Czechs declined being part of a democratized empire in the Paulskirche in 1848, and the Young Turk attempt at an Ottoman citizenship foundered and made way for a fierce Turkish nationalism.

7   Rousseau, who very early laid bare the logic of this idea, saw that a democratic sovereign couldn't just be an "aggregation," as with our lecture audience above; it has to be an "association," that is, a strong collective agency, a "corps moral et collectif" with "son unité, son *moi* commun, sa vie et sa volonté." This last term is the key one, because what gives this body its personality is a volonté générale (*Contrat Social*, book 1, chap. 6).

8   I have discussed this relation in Charles Taylor, "Les Sources de l'identité moderne," in Mikhaël Elbaz, Andrée Fortin, and Guy Laforest, eds., *Les Frontières de l'Identité: Modernité et postmodernisme au Québec* (Sainte-Foy: Presses de l'Université Laval, 1996), 347–64.

9   See Charles Taylor, "Glaube und Identität," *Transit*, no. 16 (winter 1998/1999): 21–38.

10 See José Casanova, *Public Religions in the Modern World* (Chicago: University of Chicago Press, 1994).

14 Provincializing Europe

1   Dipesh Chakrabarty, *Provincializing Europe* (Princeton: Princeton University Press, 2000).

Charles Taylor is Professor of Law and Philosophy at
Northwestern University and Professor Emeritus of
Political Science and Philosophy at McGill University.

Library of Congress Cataloging-in-Publication Data
Taylor, Charles.
Modern social imaginaries / Charles Taylor.
p. cm. — (Public planet books)
ISBN 0-8223-3255-8 (cloth : alk. paper)
ISBN 0-8223-3293-0 (pbk. : alk. paper)
1. Social sciences—Philosophy.   2. Philosophy and social
sciences.   3. Ethics.   4. Idealism.   I. Title.   II. Series.
H61.15.T39   2004   300′.1—dc22   2003014769